YOU
WILL
GET
THROUGH
THIS
NIGHT

DANIEL HOWELL

I've written this book for myself, the younger Dan that I wish could have read these pages. I hope this book can do the same for anyone who needs it.

Thank you to the friends and followers in my life that have given me patience and kindness.
I am here because of you.

YOU
WILL
GET
THROUGH
THIS
NIGHT

DANIEL HOWELL

DEY ST.
An Imprint of WILLIAM MORROW

CONTENTS

Part 1

THIS NIGHT

54

Part 2

TOMORROW

94

CONTENTS

Part 3

THE DAYS AFTER THAT

216

There's a moment at the end of every day, where the world falls away and you are left alone with your thoughts. A reckoning. When the things you have been pushing to the background come forward and demand your attention.

Mental health is something we all have. Whether you know you're going through a tough time, or feel like you are fine – it's always there, invisible, but influencing what you feel, how you react. Sometimes it can feel like a fog you're powerless to navigate through, but that's not true. You can be your own light.

It's not something to be cured, there isn't one solution, but if we understand our minds, we can communicate with our consciousness and put ourselves back in control so we can really live. So the next day you know what steps to take to make a change, and you can look after yourself the days after that. We're on this journey for a long time and we owe it to ourselves to not just survive, but thrive. I can do it and so can you.

You will get through this night.

KEEP SAFE

If you're ever at a point of serious crisis and feel like you can't keep yourself safe, it's important to connect with someone who can help you.

- Consider connecting with a friend, relative, or someone else who you trust. Even if you don't feel like talking, just being with them can be enough to keep you from harm.

- Call a crisis helpline. No matter where you are or what's happening in your life, you can connect anonymously with trained professionals who are ready to listen, in total confidence – that means no judgement.

- Go to a place of safety. This might be a hospital, police station, spiritual place, or somewhere else you feel secure.

This book tackles many topics related to mental health that some readers may, at times, find uncomfortable or upsetting as we discuss how to overcome these struggles. If you don't want to read about a particular issue, you can always skip that part, put it down, or come back when you are ready. It may be difficult, but we will talk about these things to better understand them and learn how to manage ourselves to be healthier and happier.

Introduction

Hello, I'm Dan. I might like to think of myself as tall, dark and mysterious – the truth is that whilst I am long, I'm definitely a nerd, an introvert and one of those people that spends too much time on the internet. I do only wear black though. I'm still trying to work out the psychological significance of my light-absorbing choice of clothing, but there's other stuff for me to work on first.

As an annoying child who screamed 'look at me' before doing an underwhelming backflip into a pool, naturally I wanted to become 'an entertainer'. A professional storyteller, whatever that is. Someone that can make other people laugh and maybe make a change – or at the very least have an excuse to go on a rant about something, inspired by righteous fury. I'm one of those quite sarcastic, cynical ones with a tough shell, which I always chalked up to being British, with that small and stiff upper-lip. When I was eighteen, I started posting comedy videos online to amuse myself, then people started watching them. As this accidental freight train picked up speed, with more viewers and followers coming with every rotation, I found myself (often with my friend and partner-in-crime Phil Lester) hosting a show on BBC radio, writing books, performing in theatres and standing in front of seas of people at festivals. Always self-deprecating, shamelessly sharing my worst moments for others' entertainment, (definitely to a fault and extent that sometimes elicits a laugh followed by a concerned look) – you can obviously learn a lot about my mental health from my sense of humour, but really I just want to make people happy. Other people.

I'd always been seen on a stage or a screen with a smile on my face. To everyone in my life I may have appeared fine and thriving, but under the surface I was struggling. It was easy to forget, as I tumbled forward through life, to pay attention to how I felt. I try not to think of all the time I've spent indulging in the bleakest impulses of my brain and accepting my most negative thoughts without question. I found myself wading aimlessly through a dense fog of stress, panic and low energy, which eventually sent me sliding down into a black hole that I couldn't climb out of.

I came to learn that I wasn't looking after my mental health, and in reality I was stressed, anxious and severely depressed. I went on a journey to find help, to learn about myself and my mind, and I discovered that life didn't have to be this way.

There were times in my life that seemed so dark and inescapable that I thought I had no choice but to give up entirely to escape them. The truth is that there was so much I could have done to lift myself up and out. I just didn't understand mental health, or know how to help myself. Now, I feel like I do.

THE ORIGIN STORY

From a young age, I experienced a lot of conflict, both in and outside the home. It's easy to look at two large humans shouting at each other with flailing limbs and think 'ah yes, I, the tiny child who only understands basic shapes and how to scatter Lego on the floor for people to stand on must have caused this.' The emotions

I witnessed were volatile and inconsistent. I didn't understand it, or why it was happening, so I assumed it was my fault. This led to me concluding, quite early, that this is simply how life is. So when I encountered hostility amongst the other hyperactive and impressionable children in a class, I simply accepted it and didn't push back. I had no reason to question it or that I should feel otherwise. I never really learned the concept of 'asking for help', or 'sharing feelings', so I unknowingly suffered in silence. And so, years of my life went by, unquestioning, feeling perpetually scared and hypervigilant, with a deep sinking feeling that I was ultimately unliked and a burden. This deep feeling became familiar to me. It became my normal.

As life started to get more complicated – and hormonal – the whirlwind of conflict escalated both internally and externally. Basically, I'm gay. Teen-Dan didn't have a great time with that. It was an unsurprisingly grey and generic world growing up in Winnersh – a glamorous series of housing estates built next to a motorway in the south of England. 'Gay' at that time was a synonym for bad. I realised I must be 'bad'. I felt bad. This general g-word that existed throughout the world: TV, music, the school yard – meant anything from 'boring' to 'awful', and I internalised that definition of who I was under the surface. Trying to survive the Battle Royale post-apocalypse hellscape of an all-boys school, in a society that was broadly homophobic, drilled into me that I was essentially defective. I felt guilty for being 'bad', so could not turn to anyone to talk about how I felt about this shameful part of myself. Without getting into too much traumatic detail, it was pretty terrible. Constantly outcast, tired of the constant physical and verbal abuse I suffered everywhere I turned, every day, feeling like I was fundamentally flawed and there was no escape in sight – I attempted to take my own life. Thankfully, it failed.

It turns out life can be slow, but it's long, and change is inevitable. I did not stay trapped in that environment, I did meet new people and, thankfully, the world did change, if only a little bit. To think that my story could have ended because I thought I had seen everything that was left for me in life? I was wrong. I am grateful to be alive.

At the time, no one knew of what almost happened, other than me. I carried the burden alone as another shameful secret – but now I had a mission. I told myself a story that if I could just escape, 'get a proper job' and build a life for myself, on my own terms, everything would be okay. This became a target that would define the next decade of my life. I knew my skeleton was in its own figurative closet, but there was way too much to deal with in all areas of my life to come to terms with that, so I buried it – instead choosing to just focus relentlessly on my escape plan.

It was at this time in my life, purely out of chronic boredom, that I decided to post those homemade comedy videos on the internet (absolutely horrifying please don't search), joking about things like procrastination and annoying people who walk too slowly. I found this fun, but it wasn't going to go anywhere. Surely? Despite having passionate interests in a dozen different directions, I was so convinced that I shouldn't question how I feel or the way the world works, that I decided the only plan was to play it totally traditionally and aspire to one of those jobs a grandparent would be proud of. I went

It turns out life
can be slow, but it's
long, and change
is inevitable.

to university to study Law. That sounded like a 'real job' a 'normal functional human' would get! No offence to successful lawyers who are happy with their careers, it really just was not my personal passion at any level. It was just another lie I was telling myself.

Aside from my default mindset of feeling invisible and afraid, and the bones rattling in the metaphorical wardrobe on wheels following close behind me, a new, slower and more creeping feeling started to develop within me. It was telling me that instead of the usual high-energy panic, I should just slow down and give up. Don't get out of bed. Don't eat. Don't look forward to anything, what's the point? It was the first twinges of inauthenticity starting to erode me from the inside like the acid frothing from a battery.

I decided to take a 'year out' from university to consider what to do with my life. It was during this year of staring at blank walls questioning my choices that the BBC called out of the blue, to offer Phil and me the chance to create our own show on the radio. It was happening. The thing I wanted to do! I was lost in life on so many levels, but I at least understood the importance of doing something that makes you happy, so would I finally get to experience this 'happiness' thing now? It turns out nothing slaps you down to earth quite like paying rent in London – and thusly living off Supermarket Value ramen noodles for several years. It was an exciting and incredibly stressful time. Suddenly my homemade content was opening doors and getting kinds of attention I could never imagine. In my desperation to chase the ephemeral concept of 'a career', however, I was not living a lifestyle conducive to good mental health. I didn't eat, I didn't sleep, I had no friends, I never went outside, my work was my life, my home was my work and my priorities were whack. Any down-time I had was spent face down on the carpet having an existential crisis.

This is when my life got thrown into the pit of the very new psychological phenomenon of social media. Sure, technology brings all kinds of joy and connectedness to our lives, but it can reveal the dark side of humanity along with it, and I experienced a lot of both sides. I enjoyed the middle – suddenly all these followers of my work were sending me messages, recognising me on the street, and sending me slightly creepy but well-intentioned mail. This actually made me feel accepted, appreciated and for the first time grateful that it appears there's some nice people in the world. I was thankful, it was fun! Even if someone told me, 'I went to your show and I respectfully decided I dislike you and your face,' at least it was cordial and I loved and cherished the interaction. However, as I'm sure we all now know from daily adventures on the net, it's hard to ignore the extremes. Having an encouraging cult contingency that says 'you are perfect and I will gladly kill for you' can blow up your head so big your brain is a blimp. Thankfully, my cripplingly low self-esteem never quite let me believe it. On the other hand, there were the people who decided on that particular day that I would be the sole focus of their seething rage and resentment, as all the frustration of their bad day at work was taken out on me in the DMs. Thankfully, my cripplingly low self-esteem never quite let that sink in either; I'd told myself a lot worse.

As my following grew, so did the pressures and peering gazes that were put on me. What I wasn't braced for were the invasions of privacy. I hadn't accounted for the rainbow-elephant in the room that I'd have to address one day, and that if I stumbled into a 'public career', suddenly other people would say 'hi, what's with that giant elephant you're clearly ignoring?' I was suddenly dealing with speculations on my relationship status, people trying to find evidence that I was 'lying' about who I was, the constant fear of my identity and loved ones being used as objects for entertainment or fuel for headlines.

I started to feel those same urges to escape that I'd felt as a teenager. It was too much. This clown career I'd chosen telling jokes on the internet just wasn't paying the extortionate bills. The pressure that it put on my personal life was too big to handle. I chose to take jobs that I didn't want, and do things on my own platforms that I felt were what people 'wanted to see' rather than what I was passionate about. If I wasn't doing what I wanted on my own terms now, surely I was just as much of a fraud as when I convinced myself I could be a lawyer?

I was completely caught up in the storm. Any worries that entered my mind would overwhelm me. I ceased to exist in the physical world as I was captivated by the chaotic thoughts in my head, summoning my worst memories, prophesying my own doom, imagining the enemies that I thought were waiting for me out in the world, with the worst intentions. My physical health started to deteriorate: I was tense, short of breath, tired but wired with anxious energy. Even as positive opportunities in my career started to present themselves, the pressure and attention that came with them started to boil over.

I just became a machine. Push it all under. Bury it. Head down, hide the evidence, march forward, deal with it later. 'One day' my mission will be successful: I'll reach the surface of financial freedom to secure my independence and I can take that first breath of air. After spending most of my twenties in this state of relentless chase / escape, there came a time after my first book was published, having just done a comedy world tour performing from Stockholm to LA, where surely I had finally 'made it'? I took stock of what I had – and the shelves were empty. Life was grey, much like my entire sock drawer. Even after 'achieving' what I had, I didn't have the emotional capacity to enjoy it. This initial moment, however, of really just admitting that I was not okay, gave me a spark of hope – it made me feel for the first time that I was allowed to think about my life and try to make it better.

DANIEL AND DEPRESSION

I went to a doctor, she said I might be depressed. I didn't really understand what that meant. I saw a therapist, she pointed out I clearly had several issues I probably had to deal with. I was prescribed a course of antidepressants so I could get through a day without tripping into an emotional pit, and for the first time I looked around at my world and questioned the balance. I started to try and separate work and life, actually get a hobby, find some friends – and all of this helped. It gave me a stronger foundation. Therapy helped me understand my emotional reactions and reframe my thoughts. Eventually, I found I didn't need the meds anymore. I had gone through all of this in secret, trying to keep

I just became
a machine.
Push it all under.
Bury it.

up appearances and be professional, but eventually I felt like I had to be honest about it. The people in my life and my supporters deserved to know what I was dealing with. I felt they had a right to know why I wasn't appearing as my supposedly sunnier past-self. So I decided to open up about my mental health for the first time in a video titled 'Daniel and Depression'.

The day I shared that I was suffering from depression was terrifying. Sure, I did it in my own way that poked fun at the more ridiculous sides of the struggle, carefully treading that line between letting people feel they have permission to laugh and making them wince (sorry), but the fact I was talking about this at all scared me. I didn't know whether people would understand, if they'd accept it, or if I was making a mistake admitting this vulnerability that would inevitably result in judgement. At the time 'mental health' was still a mystery to most and total taboo, so I feared I was making a mistake. I shared how I felt, explained the misconceptions of depression and how I've tried to make myself better, and braced for impact. Then people surprised me – this time, in a good way.

Sitting back looking at my screen, I saw laughter, understanding and encouragement. Old friends reached out in support. Strangers told me that they felt represented by my story and could now explain their situation to their loved ones. Some said they finally understood others in their lives that were in my position, and I realised the power of talking about these taboos and how it can help so many people.

This was the first step, but I knew there was more waiting for me on the road ahead. I'd go out on tour and people would open up to me about their struggles, emotionally sharing how I 'inspired them' by sharing 'my story' about depression, and I felt like a fraud. After all, I was still in denial about that thing I've known since I was a child. Despite my hard work to make my life better for my mental health, there was a final hurdle dragging it all down. I knew I wasn't being honest with myself and until I was living a truly authentic life, I would never be happy. I couldn't keep going any longer. I couldn't create, I couldn't perform, my body was pushing against the current of my mind, forcing me to finally confront it. It was time to go on a journey – an internal one to Narnia and back. If I wasn't living my truth, feeling happy being myself and doing things I felt passionate about, I would never be free. The time had come, to come out.

DAN 1.0

I knew that as long as I was so busy working that I had no energy left at the end of the day, I could never step back to get the perspective on my life that I needed to grow, so I took some time out. To the outside world, it probably looked like I was abducted by aliens. There were definitely a few good conspiracy theories that I must have flown over a triangle or got invited into the illuminati. The truth was that I just stopped running for the first time, and when I turned around, there was a lot waiting for me. Trying to untangle my past, like that box of miscellaneous wires that we all have at the bottom of some box, took time, but it would take as much time as I needed. After everything I'd been through, it was literally life or death.

Safe to say there was a lot going on, wading through decades of trauma while under the spotlight, but lurking at the back was the skeleton. The fundamental fact I'd been afraid to look at my whole life. I'd never been homophobic, or any kind of hateful towards others in life, but society's 'gay is bad' brainwashing that I was subjected to directed all of it inwards – in what I understand now is 'internalised homophobia'. I thought I was broken. I hated myself. I believed this bullshit to be self-evident. Recognising that this self-hatred was, in fact, not 'true', and something I could let go of, was like the first beam of light piercing straight through the clouds that had been descending on me all my life. The lightbulb moment for me was stepping back and saying 'it's okay to be the way you are.' I gave myself permission to exist. The moment I felt comfortable actually acknowledging and accepting my sexuality, and that I was ready to be honest with the world, felt like the beginning of my life.

If I was going to finally confront this, there was a lot of busy work to do just sharing the news. I learned from being open about my mental health that part of the hard work (of someone struggling with a stigma) is managing other people's emotional reactions and preparing for the bad ones, so a whole heap of fun awaited me for dropping this bombshell. I struggled so much to 'come out' to my family, that after months of procrastination, I literally just emailed them saying 'Basically I'm Gay' – which while being an unconscionably ridiculous subject line, and way too on the nose for someone as socially awkward as me, actually did the job perfectly. I then spent months in a deep hibernation cave, writing an epic and dramatic coming out comedy piece called 'Basically I'm Gay' in that email's honour. You can search for that one if you want.

The moment I shared this with the world, it actually felt like a weight lifted. I never truly understood that saying until now – it felt like my whole life had been held down by this chainmail that I instantly shed. Finally, for the first time, on a personal level, I felt free to just exist in peace moment-to-moment.

Here I am, finally living. Now what?

I've seen in the world and experienced for myself how much there is to learn about mental health. Understanding how our minds work can totally change, even save, our lives. It has personally blown my mind to learn all of the everyday behaviours I didn't appreciate were harmful, all the unhelpful attitudes I held towards myself for no reason, and what I can do to support my mental health going forward. This has helped me. I hope this book helps you, I hope it can then help others.

This is not a memoir. It's not spiritual self-help. It is a practical guide, founded on science, that can help you understand and manage your mental health. I'm just the guy who's here to make it fun along the way and say that I know working on yourself can feel like work, so if laughing at my pain can make it easier for you, I'm happy to. I'm used to it.

Just know, speaking
as someone who has
been through it all –
no matter how dark
it gets, you will get
through this night.

HOW TO USE THIS BOOK

Think of this book as a toolbox, for your mind – a metaphorical one, please leave any actual tools in your mind to the surgeons. Packed in these pages are the insights you may need to understand mental health, and practical things you can try that have been proven to make people feel better. Each small change will help build a stronger foundation for good mental health, so it is the best you vs. the world.

The proof of these pages

I'm not an expert, I'm just the guy with the laptop and a story. When anyone starts giving advice about mental health, you should be sure you can trust what they are saying. I have written this book in consultation with an experienced Clinical Psychologist – Dr Heather Bolton. All this content has been thoroughly reviewed and approved (even if I wrote ten pages and had to delete it all, much to my horror) – so trust that what made it onto these pages is thoroughly fact-checked, and hopefully entertaining.

The theory this book is based on, the exercises and advice within, come from evidence-based approaches. This means it's founded on scientific understanding of the problems, and has been tested and proven to be effective. If it's in this book, it's not just a nice sounding idea or a self-discovery, it's cold, hard science that has been shown to work. This includes approaches from CBT (Cognitive Behavioural Therapy), ACT (Acceptance and Commitment Therapy), CFT (Compassion-Focused Therapy) and Positive Psychology.

Many books are dedicated to exploring a single topic, method of treatment or mindset. These books often have a single fundamental point to make, but can then have a lot of history or methods around the answers. This is valid, but not necessarily the most useful experience for someone who needs help. This book is a lean, mean mental health machine. We'll cover many of the known and new methods understood to really make a difference – but I'll make the point you need to understand and move on to the next one. You should never rely on just one book, but this one is essentially the helpful highlights of half the library.

The small print

This is a book containing information, it isn't a sentient personal expert that will overhaul your entire life no matter the specific circumstances (genuinely sorry about that). It's up to you to take what is contained in this text and apply it to you and your life. In mental health, there are no miracle cures that work for everyone – we're all built differently and you have to find what works for you. Different experts may prefer different approaches, but they all have common ground that reveals the fundamental things that we should all know, and that's what is in here!

This book focuses on the general human experiences we all have, helping us to understand how the things we do every day affect our minds, so we can learn to manage ourselves better. Feeling bad is normal, and not always dangerous or serious. We can feel depressed or anxious without having serious diagnosable disorders and it's important to understand the line between what things this book will cover that can apply to us all, and what someone may need to seek professional help for. This is not a diagnostic textbook that will go into detail describing various conditions – we'll leave that to the professionals and dense dusty tomes. As a general rule, if you've been feeling bad for more than a couple of weeks, are struggling to cope day-to-day, or are worrying if what you're going through is 'serious enough' to need an intervention, it's worth speaking to a professional. There were times in my life where I needed more than a book, and it's important to accept that and seek help.

You aren't expected to read everything here overnight, apply all of it in one day and wake up a superhero – for many of us it's a series of small steps and changes that help us build up the strength and stamina to survive the trials of life. Read the book, see what resonates, try something out and don't be afraid. You're allowed rest days, you're allowed to forgive yourself for failure, and it's okay if something doesn't work for you. This can be on your shelf for when you need it, ready to pick up again – so that you can pick yourself up.

It's my hope that from this book you will understand how all the things we do and experience all the time affect our mental health, so we feel more informed, in control of our choices, and know how to help ourselves to live happier. This is the book I wish I could have read earlier.

The toolbox

This book is in three parts, designed to help you at different stages: from changing how you feel right now, to improving the world around you to help you feel better in a few days, to long-term attitudes and missions you can undertake to make yourself confident going forward. Think of these three parts as the previously mentioned priorities you need to address, in order to have a healthier mind. You don't need to read this cover to cover, chronologically – feel free to skip to the parts you may need right now, depending on what part of the mental health wave you're riding.

PART 1: THIS NIGHT

This part of the book is for when you need an immediate change, no matter how small. If you're in a negative headspace and need an out, This Night has techniques to help remove yourself from that negative moment. These include ways to calm down emotionally, regulate your breathing, and help to ground yourself, bringing you out of your mind and feeling safe and secure in the real world. It also has advice on how to cope with overwhelming worry or anxiety and make you steady.

PART 2: TOMORROW

This part is for when you feel stable and can make changes to the world around you. Taking a practical approach, we will go through the areas of life that we know directly affect our mental health, and for each of these areas there are easy wins that will make it simple for you to manage everything you have going on, and build momentum towards being in a sustainable, positive place.

PART 3: THE DAYS AFTER THAT

The final part builds upon the foundations and looks inside. This is about addressing what's going on in your mind, and learning to make it a better place to be. We will discuss identifying toxic thinking patterns, dealing with emotions, detecting sources of any emotional distress, and ways to adjust your mindset to deal with challenges and be fairer to yourself going forward in life.

Throughout the book, there will be a mix of the straight-up advice you need to hear, explanations of the theory behind it all (that blew my mind and made me wonder why we don't know all this stuff and teach it in schools), and my personal experiences and perspective. I know better than most that in the midst of a crisis, sometimes you don't want to read about someone's personal journey or how the researcher had their eureka moment, you just want the help – so we've designed this book to emphasise the important bits and break out the best nuggets of knowledge to make it the most helpful for you. After all, you picked this book up for a reason. By picking it up, you may have taken the first step of acknowledging that we have the ability to make ourselves feel better – and every page from here will hopefully give you help along the way. Let's get into it.

UNDERSTANDING MENTAL HEALTH

Mental health is the state of your emotional and psychological wellbeing. Just as real as your physical health, but unseen, in your mind. 'Having mental health' isn't a problem, it's just how we feel at any time. Is your mental health good, or are you struggling?

Too many of us only look at the outside when we think about how healthy we are. As long as we aren't in pain, and don't seem to be shooting blood out of some orifice, we may consider ourselves fine – but if how we feel is holding us back from doing the things we need to do or enjoying life, then we should be just as concerned with our minds.

The big difference with mental health is that we're not very good at noticing problems. We can live with a lot of stress, a lot of anxiety. Many people can function with depression. It is possible to cruise through life suffering, if we don't understand that it isn't necessary to feel this way. The first step is to understand that you feel things for a reason. Our thoughts and feelings are not a mysterious fog of frustration, they are our brain's responses to what happens in the world around us. If you understand why you feel different things, you can change how you feel. If you can change how you feel, you can feel good.

MENTAL HEALTH PROBLEMS ARE NORMAL

It's said that right now a quarter of all people experience some kind of mental health problem each year. That's a lot of people. It's not just you. People have problems. It also shows that mental health doesn't discriminate: no matter how 'successful' someone may appear in all aspects of their life, they are still as likely to experience things like depression or anxiety, as there are so many reasons mental health problems can develop.

However, even though they are so common, people don't like to talk about them. It's easy to share that you have a physical problem like a headache, less so that you are feeling stressed. Even if the physical problem is embarrassing (let's go with scandalously sexual), a shocking number of people would probably rather admit they had chlamydia or chronic constipation than depression. I mean, I would personally consider that oversharing, but the point is: mental health has a stigma around it.

Why is that? Mainly, because mental health isn't well understood by many people. Stigmas surface when people don't understand something and fear it. There's nothing to be ashamed of about feeling anxious, but for too many people bringing up the word 'anxiety' is confusing and scary. Too often we feel silently judged for sharing these vulnerabilities, as if they make us weak and are something strange and shameful, but in reality almost all of us feel these things, and there are ways we can manage and recover from them. If more people were open about how they feel, and more people understood the different mental health problems we all have and why, there wouldn't be so much stereotype and stigma. This is why we all need to understand and feel comfortable openly discussing our mental health.

Conversely, mental health problems aren't some sort of badge of honour and suffering isn't aspirational. Sure, the right kind of humour about shared experiences can help people to feel they aren't alone in what they are going through, and take the seriousness out of some struggles. I love an inappropriate depression joke. Laughing at how I used to literally struggle to get out of bed is probably problematic, but it actually puts me at ease and helps me make light of (and sense of) a really hard time in my life. This doesn't mean I stopped trying to get better. Don't settle on mental health problems being a part of who you are – they are challenges that you can overcome.

01101001 01110100 00100000 01101001 01110011 01101110 00100111 01110100 **IT ISN'T BINARY** 00100000 01100010 01101001 01101110 01100001 01110010 01111001

Mental health problems don't just pop up suddenly out of nowhere, like a giant rolling boulder could suddenly pop up and be a real problem for your physical health. You don't fall out of bed one morning with crippling depression, having never felt like you had a problem in your life. This is why prevention is better than a cure – just like taking vitamins or avoiding flimsy rope bridges prevents physical illness or injury, we should be able to tell when our mental health is going downhill and do something about it before hitting a crisis.

It's not something we should only notice when we are struggling: it's something we should be aware of and looking after all the time.

The good news is, your mental health is absolutely not fixed in stone. If you feel bad now, it does not mean you will stay like this forever. For every person on the planet, mental health fluctuates. No one is fine all the time. Think of it as a spectrum going from barely surviving at one end to totally thriving at the other. When we're thriving we feel happy, we're growing, we're engaging

If you're struggling,
you need to know how
to pick yourself up.
If you're thriving,
you need to
understand why.

with the world around us, feeling full of purpose and effortlessly dealing with challenges that come along the way. On the surviving end we barely function, feeling detached from the world and the people around us, struggling to maintain our physical health and keep ourselves afloat. I've had times in my life where I felt at the top of the mountain, times right at the bottom where I thought I'd never see the light again, and a whole lot of time on an average emotional rollercoaster in the middle. I want a refund from this theme park.

The reality is most of us are in the middle of this spectrum most of the time. Life isn't without its challenges, but we can usually rise to them and, depending on all the factors in and out of our control, stay balanced as we ride the waves. However, many factors in life are totally within our control, and with the help of this book, you can take charge of them and make a real difference to how you feel. If you're struggling, you need to know how to pick yourself up. If you're thriving, you need to understand why and know how to keep yourself there going forward.

GET YOUR PRIORITIES STRAIGHT

There's no point trying to reach enlightenment if you're being actively chased by a tiger. In Psychology there are many theories describing the 'needs' we have in life and their order of importance. Basically, you can't try to tackle new aspirational goals if you're still being nibbled by the aforementioned tigers – sorry, problems in your life. Our first (and very basic) priorities to survive as humans are food, water, sleep and safety. If we are fundamentally safe, our problems will be mental. Are we coping and feeling content? Or, are our minds now preventing us from basic functioning, and enjoying our day-to-day lives? I guess if you've completely mastered both physical health and mental health, at some point you magically transcend consciousness and float between states across space and time as an eleventh-dimensional brain, shooting lasers of peace and wisdom from your temporal lobe – but, personally, my brain is more occupied randomly resurfacing the cringe-inducing memory of when I tripped into a teacher's boob when I was 13, so write to me if you ever get there.

Being a human

If you understand the things that shape who you are, it can explain a lot and be reassuring to know that we're all in the same mess. We can broadly box our relationship with mental health into being shaped by the following things:

SOCIAL ENVIRONMENT

Both the environment you grew up in and the one you're in now. As a child, how you were treated, if you were praised or criticised, smothered or neglected. Your circumstances in life, such as where you were born, struggling for money, suffering adversity for who you are, and any traumatic experiences. And now, things like your home life, how well supported you feel by the people around you, how safe you feel, and wider things like culture and the state of politics – all adding up to form the experience you've learned from in life. If an aspect of your identity or upbringing makes life in this world harder, it can understandably impact your mental health.

BIOLOGY

From the outset we are given advantages or disadvantages. We inherit genetic blueprints from our parents, they shape the unique way our bodies respond to stress, the amount of sleep we personally need to function, and the chemical reactions inside of us that affect everything from nutrition to medication. It's different for everyone. At various points in our lives, from puberty to menopause and beyond, we are at the mercy of hormones pulling us wildly in different directions – and our chemical balances can also be influenced by various medications. If you naturally wake up full of energy in the morning, and have a fast metabolism, for example, I may hate you?

PSYCHOLOGY

The mindset through which you approach life. We all have personal philosophies, views of the world, and values that affect our ability to solve problems, deal with confrontation and learn new skills. We can be held back by past traumas and have different levels of resilience, coping skills, and ways of dealing with strong emotions.

These aspects combine to create a story that is unique to you. For example, I love to criticise myself constantly (Psychology), so when I encounter setbacks in life (Social Environment) I am more likely to blame myself or eternally dwell on my failure. Or, if I get no sleep because I've been contemplating doom until 3 a.m. (Psychology), I have no energy (Biology) and I struggle to find joy in my hobbies and friendships and struggle to cope with the tasks in my day. I am a human.

These different aspects may explain your disposition, but you are more than the sum of these parts. We all get dealt different cards, and end up in different places in life; there are things we can do to take control and make our minds what we want them to be. This book will focus on the things that are changeable – so just remember you may be a product of what made you, but you have the power to change and grow and make yourself feel better. And you are not the only one.

You may be a product of what made you, but you have the power to change and grow and make yourself feel better.

Blame evolution

So many of our unhelpful habits, emotions and natural reactions to situations are leftovers from six million years ago when we were stressed apes. On one hand, perhaps we should be grateful that they survived multiple ice ages for us, but they left us with in-built responses for ancient solutions that affect our modern mental problems.

The main purpose of our brain's evolution was to prevent us from getting harmed. Our incredible great-grand-ancestors were under constant threat from giant birds and moderate weather, so their brains had to be very emotionally reactive – where any negativity or threat was probably a life-or-death situation that had to send their bodies into stress or panic to deal with the danger. Nowadays, we're much safer in general, but we still have the primitive-threat-detection system installed that kicks in whenever we get given a deadline, or try to pass a stranger crossing a street and can't decide which side we're going around for a continuous minute. This, combined with a more recently developed part of the brain that loves to overthink, dwell on problems and converse with ourselves (mostly criticising) means sometimes our brains are not helping. Just know that if you ever jump to a worst case scenario, or feel a full-body convulsion coming on from a random thought, it's not necessarily a real threat, your primordial fish-brain thinks it's a giant shark – blame evolution. Understanding the difference between how your brain wants you to feel, and the reality of your situation, is fundamental to taking charge of your mental health.

Horrible helpful feelings

You will never free yourself from feelings, and you shouldn't want to; some are quite nice. Instead of repressing or trying to rid yourself of the unpleasant ones, we should instead learn to understand them and be comfortable living with them.

Anxiety is what we experience when we perceive a threat, and it's a normal and necessary emotion. It can range from a casual worry to an all encompassing fear of a future danger – so it can scale from an ominous presence in the background to an overwhelming feeling of doom. The feeling of worry or panic is very uncomfortable, but if we understand that it's a natural reaction to stress and threat, we can be less scared of it.

The 'anxiety response' is hard-wired into us, and probably responsible for the survival of our species. For something that ruins so many otherwise lovely afternoons of mine, it's quite an impressive bit of design that I can at least appreciate the idea behind.

When we perceive a threat, our brain triggers an immediate emotional and physical response that prepares us to run, fight, or freeze. Fight, flight, or like a deer in a light, just fright. Our brain might not instantly know how we want to solve a situation, so it just hits the alarm bell, setting off a series of emotional and physical responses so we're ready for anything. Being actively chased by a tiger, you might need your body to run very fast, so a nervous sweat keeps you cool, and your bowels want to evacuate for that extra speed advantage. If you go for the fight (brave and commendable), an increased heart-rate pumps blood into your muscles. Or maybe your brain just wants you to be super-scared of the looming orange threat and play dead, which explains why we sometimes react by freezing in the midst of a trauma – it can be a very adaptive safety response. (People often say this strategy works for bears? Based on what I've seen from domesticated cats, freezing would lead to total annihilation in a tiger scenario.)

The problem now is obviously we're not regularly being mauled by sabre-toothed predators. We get the same reaction from the threat of public speaking, the aftermath of an awkward moment, or even just imagining a stressful situation. The alarm bells will ring and our bodies will do their thing.

Sometimes our bodies' natural reactions to these feelings are so strong we can misinterpret them as being dangers to our physical health. We could feel like our heart pounding as we're standing still is a heart attack, or sudden shortness of breath means we're suffocating. Thank you, body auto-pilot, very helpful.

The key thing to remember is that these bad feelings themselves are not dangerous. Although it feels horrible, anxiety can't actually harm you. Only the tiger can. We don't want to rid ourselves of the acute ways our brain keeps us out of danger and motivates us to do things, but we can understand it better and learn to tame it. Do you see? The real tiger was inside you all along. I'm sorry.

SYMPTOM	FEELS LIKE	BIOLOGICAL EXPLANATION
Racing heart	I'm having a heart attack	Heart beating faster to pump more blood around the body
Dizziness	I'm going to faint	Blood pressure rises to help heart pump blood[1]
Tight chest	I can't breathe	Muscles of body contracting and tightening to be ready for action
Short of breath	I'll suffocate	Rapid, shallow breathing to increase oxygen in the blood and aid quick thinking
Trembling or shaking	I'm going to collapse	Muscles are getting ready for action
Tunnel vision or blurred vision	I can't see	Pupils dilate to allow more light in; vision focuses on danger and minimises distractions
Butterflies in stomach	I'm going to be sick	Blood leaving the stomach to pause digestion and move to limbs
Urge to go to the bathroom	I'm about to have a terrible, terrible accident	Body wants to get rid of unwanted weight to aid fighting/running[2]
Excessive sweating	I'm overheating	Body keeping cool[3]
Blood drains from face / skin surface	I look ill	Blood going to vital organs away from places it's not needed. Also reduces the risk of losing blood through the skin if bitten by a predator!

1 It's actually impossible to faint due to anxiety, as your blood pressure increases when you're anxious, whereas we faint due to low blood pressure
2 One way to distract during a fight
3 Also sweating makes your skin more slippery so it's harder for a predator to grip hold of you – I guess sweaty wrestlers are cheating

Of course, this being said, if you aren't feeling catastrophically stressed or anxious and you experience these symptoms, you might actually be having a medical emergency. Use your brain. Please go to see a doctor.

DON'T PANIC

In moments of overwhelming anxiety, our reaction to our bodies' natural physical responses can swell into a panic attack. Panic attacks often seemingly come out of nowhere with no apparent explanation, which makes them rather alarming, but can also be triggered by situations such as being faced with a phobia. Panic attacks can be a one off for someone during a particularly stressful moment. For some, they may happen more often, and a fear of further attacks can seriously dent confidence in going outside or putting yourself in other similar situations again – this can be referred to as panic disorder or develop into agoraphobia.

Panic attacks can, understandably, be quite stressful. If you suddenly feel like you can't breathe or that your heart is malfunctioning, it will inevitably lead to more anxiety, which will bring more physical symptoms which pile up, feeding the 'panic cycle', which can feel incredibly dangerous. The natural instinct is often to gasp for air, which only puts our bodies on higher alert, makes it more difficult to breathe and causes dizziness which isn't good for feeling mental clarity. That stereotypical image of someone on the floor breathing into a paper bag? Yes, that is an absolutely terrible idea. They need to breathe slowly and gently, not sharply inhale the sugar from the bottom of someone's bag of popcorn.

In the midst of a panic attack, there's often also the social fear of judgement, or needing to suddenly find a safe place, which can compel you to run and hide. Choosing to escape the anxiety-inducing situation can allow immediate relief, but can also just reinforce the fear in the longer term, when actually the situation that sparked the anxiety was probably not physically dangerous – but now it's extra scary.

Panic attacks subside quite quickly, usually peaking in intensity within around five to ten minutes and ending within twenty. Granted, twenty minutes of panic where you fear the absolute worst may feel a lot longer, but they don't last forever. Common methods of 'grounding' yourself include stomping on the floor, or feeling running water to distract you. If you have a panic attack, allow yourself some time to recover, as even if you logically recognise you're fine, your body probably needs to come down from high alert and your emotions deserve a break too. Just know – it isn't abnormal or concerning for your health or sanity to have panic attacks. It's a perfectly reasonable reaction to what your body is sending you.

In Part 1 of this book, we will go over techniques to manage anxiety and be present that can help if you find yourself in this situation.

OUT OF BODY EXPERIENCE

Another common, but deeply unsettling response to anxiety, is **dissociation** which can take different forms – sometimes just feeling like you're 'zoning out' from reality. **Derealisation** is that feeling of being detached from your surroundings, or as if things around you are foggy or unreal. It can feel like being in a hazy dream where you can't wake up. **Depersonalisation** is where you feel you aren't physically in your body, but observing it. This sense that you're losing touch with reality is, understandably, quite horrifying. It can be extremely alarming the first time you experience it, but it is often actually a harmless (in itself) symptom of anxiety that most people will experience at some point, and often passes quickly.

During an episode of derealisation, people often panic that this means they are developing psychosis, or losing control of their mind in a serious, permanent way – but this is not the case. It's natural in one of these moments to search for an explanation, and not being able to find a clear one can bring even more anxiety, making it more overwhelming. The main thing to remember is that short episodes aren't generally unusual or serious.

We can also experience dissociation as a consequence of trauma – our brains trying to disconnect from something upsetting, as a protective mechanism. If it's something that you struggle to recover from, or keeps recurring often, it can be worth talking to a professional to explore what's underpinning it.

I've had moments of dissociation before incredibly stressful exams as a teenager, sat around a particularly chaotic and argumentative holiday family dinner table – even sometimes after positive, but quite overwhelming moments when I've performed on stage. Many events in life can cause our thoughts to reach a point of chaos where our brains overload, but as long as we understand why this happens and what it means, it can hopefully go from a distressing mental mystery to a rather boring biological reaction.

ANNOYING POPUPS

At any moment, your brain is popping random thoughts into your head. Some of these are relevant to life, 'remember to buy toilet paper!' Some are completely useless, 'remember the boob-tripping incident?' Sometimes, the random thoughts in our mind can, seemingly out of nowhere, be violent, sexual, or otherwise completely shocking to ourselves. A particularly god-fearing childhood friend of mine at community youth theatre (those poor parents) used to tell me how she couldn't stop thinking blasphemous phrases. She'd be in the middle of some improv, pretending to be a personified spoon, and her brain would go 'DAMN, HECK, DARN, GOD, JESUS, TITS' – how horrifying. Straight to hell for you Jess!

These are called **intrusive thoughts**. They are something we all experience. Just because for some reason during dinner you imagined your grandparents having sex, doesn't mean you wanted to think that. You really, really, really did not want to think that . . . which is why your brain thought it. The trouble is when we get preoccupied with them, or get into a cycle where we dare our minds to summon more troubling, dark thoughts as we're so desperate to escape them. It's tempting to focus on a thought like this when it appears in your mind, and wonder if it means you are a pervert, or an aspiring murderer – but know that you are not, hopefully. Any effort to shout over your own brain or do something to prove you aren't your intrusive thought is an overcompensation. The best thing is to simply accept that our weird minds are just like this: let the intrusive thoughts come, let them pass, don't judge yourself and don't give them the attention that makes them stronger. Kind of like wasps, wasps of the mind that look like procreating elderly people killing each other. Let them buzz around and eventually they will get bored.

THE BIG D

No, not 'Dan' – thank you. Depression. A word that I know very well has a million different meanings depending on who you ask. Feeling depressed is more than feeling sad: sadness is the opposite of happiness, an emotion we usually easily understand the cause of and that doesn't hugely impact our ability to function. Sadness is usually a reaction to a loss, or that animated movie supposedly created for children but that deliberately manipulates nostalgia to make anyone over the age of thirteen cry a lake. Depression is less of an emotion you understand, but a physical feeling that may not have a recognisable cause. A pressure weighing down on you, draining your energy.

Depression can take many forms, and can range from mild to severe, and everyone will experience it in their own way. To 'feel depressed' is to feel almost emotion*less*, sometimes struggling to gather the enthusiasm to perform your basic tasks as a person or to do the things you usually enjoy. It can take away your appetite, and impact your sleep. It's not that you want to cry, you probably don't want to do anything at all. The world seems desaturated. Depression can make it hard for a person to have perspective on their position and the negative thoughts can compound and reinforce each other: 'I'm worthless', 'everything I do will fail', 'life is pointless'. Sometimes depression can start to make someone believe that their life isn't worth living, or that there's no way out of their situation, potentially putting them at risk of harming themselves.

For a long period of my life, I simply thought this was my normal. I didn't question how I felt, so when I was told by a doctor I may be depressed, I was honestly shocked at the implication that my mental health was something I had any influence over. If you recognise these symptoms in yourself, please question it, as I wish I had sooner.

The common (obnoxiously irritating) misconception about depression is that someone can just get over it in the same way they would just feeling sad, by 'getting up' and shaking it off with a little dance, a cheeky chocolate bar or smelling some flowers. Granted, laughter is a great medicine in mental health for boosting a mood! It won't fix the fundamental causes of the condition, but as a plaster it can perk someone up. I personally always appreciated

For a long period of my life, I simply thought this was my normal.

someone making an effort to make a joke in poor taste at my expense, my friends knew I'd appreciate the morbidity and it would give me some perspective to push me through the day. I appreciate my sense of humour may not be normal and something a Psychologist could write a book on in itself.

There are a few explanations for depression. Sometimes it is a chemical imbalance, a lack of the 'happy' neurotransmitter serotonin in your brain. Sometimes it's a natural consequence of grief or a trauma. Sometimes it's linked to biological changes in our bodies, like after having a baby, recovering from a major illness or adapting to a new disability. And sometimes there's no obvious explanation – if we struggle to maintain good mental health, we can slide into a depressed state without realising when or why.

An episode of depression can last a few weeks or can go on for many months or years. No two people's experiences will be the same and different approaches to treatment will work for different people.

This book aims to cover general mental health in a way that's relevant for everyone, but if the description above resonates with you, please consider seeing a professional. Depression is highly treatable, through therapy or medication (that we will discuss later in the book), so you needn't suffer alone. The advice and exercises in each part of this book will aim to give you an understanding of mental health, and tools to manage yours, to keep the black dogs at bay and keep you afloat. Look at me – after everything I've gone through, right now, I'm swimming.

Hopefully now mental health seems slightly less mysterious. It's something all of us know far too little about, considering how it dominates our experience in life. Just remember: there's a reason for all the things you think and feel. We all have the same brains, with the same range of emotions. It's perfectly normal to have problems and, most importantly, there are things you can do to make yourself feel better.

The right attitude

So let's get into action. Whatever you're going through – whether you're feeling stressed and anxious right now, or just want to set yourself up for better mental health in the long term, hopefully this book will have something to help you. Before our journey begins, here are some ground rules:

- **Be open minded.** Give yourself permission to try new things and make changes. Approach them knowing it's to make your life better.

- **Be fair to yourself.** As someone with impossibly high standards for myself, I can tell you it's unhelpful. Don't consider yourself a failure, but a work in progress. Self-compassion isn't indulgent, it's being fair and makes you more likely to succeed.

- **Be proud of yourself.** Celebrate the small wins along the way and measure yourself by your effort, not your achievements. If you are feeling low in life, things will feel harder, so rather than focus on the outcome and feeling down, feel proud that you are trying. Find hope and motivation.

- **Be brave.** Aim to push yourself out of your comfort zone just a little – that's usually where the breakthroughs happen. If something's hard, be prepared to practice and push through to the other side. If something scares you, head towards it in case there's truth and growth on the other side.

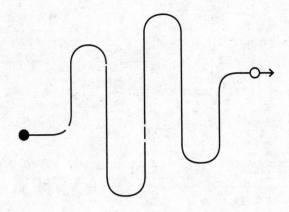

Part 1

THIS
NIGHT

Part 1

THIS NIGHT

This part is for when you are feeling bad and need an immediate change. Things to help you in the moment, so you can cope with overwhelming negative feelings.

Key thoughts to lock in your mind during a crisis:

1. Things always feel worse in the middle of the night.
In the dark, lonely hours, our minds race as we're separated from the distractions of the world. Resetting to the morning is a powerful solution. Don't make decisions based on how you feel then, as it's almost guaranteed you won't feel the same the next day. Get through the moment and look at things with fresh eyes later.

2. Feeling bad right now doesn't mean feeling bad forever.
Emotions fade away, harmful thoughts get less powerful with time and bad memories become more distant as you move forward. Change is inevitable, the bad time won't last.

3. You are not your thoughts.
This is the big one. Just because you think something, doesn't mean it's real. If you're thinking that something will be a disaster, or that people don't like you – these thoughts just come from feelings, they aren't necessarily facts.

Just because you think something, doesn't mean it's real.

Having a relatable meltdown

We all have different thresholds for how much distress we can tolerate, and when our limit gets breached, we start to feel overwhelmed.

I have the strange superpower of being incredibly resilient, which came from me being forced to adapt to stressful situations in my whacky and traumatising queer childhood, but sometimes I forget what a normal human is supposed to tolerate as I instantly categorise and compartmentalise the stressful situation I'm in, while my friends are having a two-hour tantrum. Random example: I was on tour, having just landed in Manila, and the Philippines government confiscated all the professional theatre tech our crew needed for performing our show for no apparent reason. No one was speaking to us and we were locked in an interrogation room for hours. We ended up having to cancel a show thousands of people had travelled across Asia to attend, but also couldn't publicly explain the situation in case we got arrested. I accepted what I couldn't control, put it aside, and went into problem-solving mode – while everyone else was pulling their hair out. In hindsight, I'm definitely weirdly resilient (which comes with its baggage) and it would have been perfectly reasonable to pull my hair in solidarity with everyone else.

It's normal to feel overwhelmed. From feeling unbelievably stressed by your day, to overpowering anxiety in the face of a situation, or sadness so deep you can feel it weighing down your bones. Whether you've had bad luck recently, or are still carrying the baggage from a past traumatic incident – sometimes a series of unfortunate events stack up to the point where we panic and feel like we're spiralling out of control. It's not nice, but it's also not abnormal.

I've had days when I've felt so overwhelmed I genuinely considered running away to live in a remote shack (I'd give myself three days without WiFi). I've had moments of terror about the imagined worst-case scenarios of a decision that have cost me opportunities, sending me down different paths in life. Also my exceptional ability to constantly self-doubt makes everything from making my bed, to writing a joke, a slow and painful experience.

Our minds tend to run at a million miles an hour (actually, I just verified: brain signals are between 150–270 mph. I'm definitely on the slow end). At any moment in our stream of consciousness, there is bound to be a whole waterfall of fears and criticisms. Our problem-solving brains constantly want to focus on the negatives to 'fix' them, but don't take time to appreciate what's going well, so we get stuck in a loop, like a dog being genuinely upset that it can't bite its own tail.

The natural instinct is to try to run away from moments of overwhelming emotion, but many theories demonstrate that our instinct to avoid confronting the issue and press on with a smile is counter-productive. Successfully coping isn't about avoiding bad feelings, but learning how to work with them. If we can learn to understand and react differently to our feelings, we can stop them dictating our lives.

NAVIGATING THIS NIGHT

This book has been designed for you to jump to any section that most appeals to you or you feel you need right now. The exercises in each section are practical things you can do to shift your headspace and positively manage your feelings.

For each exercise we will go through what it does and why it works so you know what to try yourself – whether your priority is calming your anxiety, stopping a rain of negative thoughts in your mind, or finally getting to sleep.

Different people like different methods – decide what works for you and trust your gut. If something makes you feel safe and calm, remember that and it becomes a weapon in your self-care arsenal.

FINDING CALM

If you need to feel calm, to get to a slower, more manageable state, there are exercises to slow your body and settle your mind – so you're ready to tackle your problems in the right headspace.

You are now aware of your own breathing

One of the main focuses of many calming exercises is breathing. I always used to be annoyed by someone making me aware of my own breathing – reading this now you probably snapped out of whatever natural rhythm you had going on, and feel like a baby animal that's completely forgotten how to regularly function. Now, however, I thank that annoying person, as breathing is one of the most fundamentally important things to understand, in order to control both how you mentally think and physically feel. If you notice you're starting to spiral, using your breathing to increase oxygen levels, reduce your heart rate and focus your mind, can instantly calm you down.

Somewhere in the woods there are a bunch of yoga people who will tell you that mastering breathing will allow you to climb a frozen mountain in a pair of Speedos, or juggle bowls of nails – and whilst that may appear to be true, we don't all need to be quite that masterful; just a bit of practice will make a big difference. When we're stressed, our brains flip into simple-mode to manage the load and respond in a more emotional, reactive way. When our brains are relaxed, we can think and behave more rationally – and even if things are falling apart around us, we will be better poised to solve the problems than if we're breathing heavily into a paper bag and knocking into furniture. Exhale.

Abdominal breathing

Sometimes I look in the mirror and feel like I definitely don't have abs, but they are there, it's a thing, and they are related to breathing.

When stressed or anxious we tend to take short, shallow breaths that come directly from the chest. You might not be aware of it, but this keeps your body in an ongoing state of stress, so you're always switched on and hyper-alert. Great for ancient-you running back to the cave to dodge the sudden lightning storm, less so for now-you when you're running late, sitting on a bus nervously twitching. Sharp breaths can make you panic, feel like you're not getting enough air, and prevent you from falling asleep.

Instead, if you breathe deeply down into your abdomen, you will engage your body's natural soothing system and create a sense of calm and safety. This is the kind of breathing that you do in deep sleep, and that newborn babies do. Stupid babies, feeling all safe in their tiny boots without a worry in the world. It's easy for them. We need to remember to make an effort.

You can understand this now by putting one hand on your chest and one on your abdomen. (Find a table or someone with a flat head to balance this book on.) Take a breath and you will notice whether your chest or stomach is inhaling more of the breath. How do you feel?

It's good to remember that no matter what is happening and where you are, your breath is always with you. It's something you can always count on to feel better.

EXERCISE: ABDOMINAL BREATHING

Good for:
- **Calming down**
- **Easing stress**
- **Feeling less anxious**

First, empty your lungs of air by gently breathing out.

Now, breathe in quietly through the nose for four seconds. Keep your shoulders relaxed when you're doing this. Try to breathe right into your belly and feel it expand.

Hold the breath for a count of four seconds.

Now exhale slowly through your mouth, slightly blowing the air out, but keeping your jaw relaxed – try to make this last around eight seconds.

The key is to ensure your exhale is longer than your inhale.

Repeat this pattern: in through the nose for four, hold for four, then slowly out through the mouth for eight.

After a few rounds, you should start to feel a state of relaxation.

Notice when you're starting to feel anxious or stressed, and adapt your breathing this way – when you activate your soothing system you'll trigger the feeling of deep physical relaxation in the body, and feel calmer and more in control.

BACK TO THE PRESENT

These next exercises focus on being in the present. Usually, negative thoughts running through your mind are either: ruminating over things that happened in the past, or worrying about what might happen in the future. Dwelling on the past can lead you to feel depressed, and panicking about the future makes you anxious. Learning to focus your mind in the moment, and simply *be*, is a powerful technique for managing your mental health.

By using our five senses (reminder, because I went blank and needed one: taste, touch, smell, sight and sound) we can ground ourselves, and from focusing on our surroundings, distract from worrying thoughts and instead feel comfortable just vibing in the moment.

I'm someone that is guilty of spending too much time 'in my head', and in the process I imagine myself looking dazed, sitting with my eyes open as my mind races between things I regret and what could go wrong ahead of me. Either constantly feeling woeful about some distant decision, like taking out a hefty student loan only to drop out of Law School to pursue comedy, or worrying about a crisis in the future, like if one day I will stop being funny, and wish that I'd pursued a more reliable career in Law. Remembering to ground myself, be present and spend more time enjoying the world around me, rather than ignoring it and living in a cloud of my own thoughts, is an essential skill.

This technique isn't about distracting yourself, though, or about calming an overactive thinker – it's about just learning to be calm in the present, without your thoughts taking your focus, empowering you to take control. Like with breathing, you can do this anytime, anyplace, but there's no time like the present.

Self-soothing

We learn how to self-soothe when we're very young, right from the start as babies. It's the ability to recognise that we feel bad, and either comfortably accept it, or do something about it, instead of just sitting there upset and distressed. When babies cry, someone usually jumps in quickly to soothe them. Maybe by rocking them, patting their back or making bizarre noises and disturbing faces, which for some reason babies already know is weird and ridiculous and rightfully laugh at. As babies grow older, they learn how to calm themselves down without a mysterious giant intervening to pick them up, by doing something or just dealing with it. This process of learning how to recognise how we feel, then making ourselves feel better, is huge.

If we don't learn to self-soothe when we're young, or if we experience trauma in our lives, we can find it hard to soothe ourselves as adults when we're upset. This can mean that feelings, rather than signalling an issue for us to solve, can take over our brains and be overwhelming. In this case, when we're upset we can look for that soothing feeling in other places, such as harmful behaviours or substances.

One of the best ways to learn self-soothing is to nurture your five senses. Tuning into your senses helps you to be present in your own body, helping you feel safe, calm and in control.

EXERCISE: SELF-SOOTHING USING YOUR FIVE SENSES

Good for:
- **Calming down**
- **Feeling safe**
- **Quieting stressful thoughts**

By tuning in to and indulging the individual senses, we focus on the physical world, rather than what's in our heads. Choose one sense to begin with:

Touch

Touching causes our brains to release chemicals that make us feel safe. By being comfortable where we are, with what we're wearing and interacting with, we quickly change our experience of reality. Try stretching, comfy clothes, blankets, warm showers, or even playing with something in your hands – any little toy (for me right now: an impossibly tangled charging cable) that you interact with can help you to remember that you are a physical object, not just the manifestation of a storm of stressful thoughts.

Vision

Looking at things that calm you down can soothe you. I'm giving you permission right now to just look at some dog images. It's not procrastination; it's serious self-soothing. Even if it's focusing on the view from your window, some art, or a film with beautiful cinematography, looking at something you know or something that pleases you, distracts your mind, and makes you feel content.

Hearing

Hearing is a very commanding way to shift our attention out of our heads. You can immediately change how you're thinking by listening to your favourite music, or someone's voice, for example, and focusing on it. Just make sure that what you are listening to will put you in the mood you want to be in. Setting off a blaring fire alarm might distract you, but not make you feel better.

Smell

We adjust to the smell of our environment very quickly, so inhaling something new is often a spark of interest. Find something with a smell that comforts you, whether it's flowers, food, or your favourite old blanket (that might actually be a bit manky but I won't judge you). There's a reason why I'm a serial hoarder of scented candles. It's a good twenty-minute meditation tour for me, just sniffing them all. Either that or I'm getting slightly high off the fumes. Either way, it works.

Taste

Really savour the taste of your favourite foods. We're too often in a rush to slam a snack down our throats, but taking time to slowly appreciate a taste is great. A hot drink that forces well-paced, appreciative sips is perfect – unless you're like my mum who goes from teapot to cup to mouth and out of the front door in ten seconds. Don't be like her. Even chewing gum can stick you to reality!

Remember that wherever you are, you can give yourself a mental break by indulging your senses. And if for a moment you feel like you don't deserve these comforts – stop that thought. You need to be in the best mental space you can to tackle life's challenges, so suffering is unsurprisingly unhelpful. Go sniff that candle.

54321

When You Need to Bring Your Mind Back to the Present

If you are feeling quite distressed, and need to quickly bring yourself back down to earth, you can combine your senses with a focused countdown to simplify your thoughts and ground yourself quickly, acknowledging each sense with more attention, counting down to calm.

EXERCISE: 54321 TECHNIQUE

Good for:
- **Dealing with overwhelming anxiety**
- **Stopping thoughts spinning**
- **Calming down quickly**

Before you begin, take a couple of deep, slow breaths so you feel ready to relax, then start tuning into each of your five senses.

5: Acknowledge FIVE things you see around you. Take time to notice your immediate area. What colours and shapes do you see? What textures are the materials? What small details like reflections of light do you see? Focus on each of these things.

4: Acknowledge FOUR things you can touch. These could be your feet in your socks, a ring on your finger, the firmness of a seat, or the texture of your clothes against your skin. Try picking up an object and exploring its weight and texture.

3: Acknowledge THREE things you hear. These might be sounds close to you, like a clock ticking, or far away, like traffic. Really try to tune in to sounds that your mind has tuned out. Don't judge these sounds and worry about them, just recognise them.

2: Acknowledge TWO things you can smell in the air around you. If you can't smell anything, bring to mind two of your favourite smells, or tune in to very subtle fragrances, even the scent of your own skin.

1: Acknowledge ONE thing you can taste. This might be gum, or even your own tongue (hopefully you've made good non-fermented choices). If you can't taste anything, try to imagine the taste of one of your favourite meals.

Take another nice slow, deep breath into your belly and notice the relaxation it brings.

Repeat this process as many times as you like. Each time you do it, notice how you feel afterwards.

This may seem slightly intense or silly if you're feeling fine and don't need it, but if you do need a quick fix to calm yourself down, this focused way to concentrate on your senses can get you there with speed.

It's intense to be tense

So many of us are constantly tense without realising. Right now I bet half the people reading this sentence are clenching their jaw, or shrugging their shoulders up into a cramp. Stop that. If we feel stressed, we often tense our bodies up and forget to relax (even hours later) and this has a profound effect on how we can feel. If you're finding it hard to calm down, sleep, or enjoy things, scan your body and be aware of any tension you find. Honestly, it's exhausting holding all that energy. Let's get loose.

To do a full-body tension-scan, you go from your toes right up to your head, tensing the muscles, then releasing. Not just feeling the tension relax away, but taking time to really acknowledge and feel your body. This is not only instantly calming, but also very helpful for grounding and focusing your thoughts in the present. Just don't clench either set of cheeks too much; if you're hurting yourself, you are literally trying to relax too hard and you're going to burst something. Chill.

EXERCISE: PROGRESSIVE MUSCLE RELAXATION

Good for:
- **Getting rid of physical tension**
- **Feeling grounded**
- **Relaxing**

Find a quiet place, comfortable and not too bright. Get as comfortable as you can, sitting or even lying down, and close your eyes if that feels comfortable.

Start with a gentle deep breath through your nose, and notice the feeling of air travelling through your lungs and across your body. Hold this breath for a few seconds, and as it releases, start to feel some tension leave your body. Repeat as much as you need, feeling tension float away with the air.

Let your breathing return to normal. Tense your toes, curl them, flex the arch of each foot and, with each breath, release the tension from this part of your body. Notice the new feeling of relaxation this brings. Slowly work up your legs, focusing on each area – tensing, releasing, breathing, feeling the oxygen in your blood run through your relaxed muscles. You may feel heavier and more connected to your body.

As you get to your torso, tense your abs for a few seconds, really squeezing, then relax and allow your body to go limp. With your back, bring your shoulders together. With your shoulders, bring them up to your ears and gently squeeze.

Now for your arms, make a fist and tense your arm all the way up to your shoulder, then release it. For your neck and head, tense your face, clench your jaw, close your eyes tight, and when you let go, welcome the wave of calmness it brings.

Finally, tense your whole body for a few seconds, then go limp. Enjoy your state of calm, relaxation and connection. When you're ready, slowly move each part of your body, give your limbs a gentle shake and you are done. Now, if I almost fell asleep writing this, you know it's going to help you relax and feel calm.

Mindfulness

Mindfulness is one of the most fundamentally important things to understand if you want to feel in control of your brain and the things it sends you. It also has to be one of the most popular words in the 'world of mental health', meditation and strangely expensive apps. It is not, as I initially guessed, a competition of how full your mind is with unhelpful thoughts that get in the way of enjoying life – if it was then I would win.

Mindfulness is a practice based on ancient Zen Buddhist techniques, but don't be scared, you don't have to climb up to a mountain temple or forego your stress-inducing modern possessions in order to benefit from the idea. There's evidence that mindfulness can help cope with stress, recurring depression, chronic pain, and even boost your creativity, memory, and concentration. So no matter how you feel, it is definitely worth learning.

It's not about stopping thoughts, or trying to have a totally blank mind, it's about allowing thoughts to arise and letting them be there. But rather than focusing on the thoughts, we focus on the world around us, or our breathing instead.

The idea is to detach and distance yourself from the thoughts that come into your mind. When a troubling thought pops into your head, instead of listening to it and letting it lead you down a path of worry, try to just accept that you had that thought – and instead of indulging in it or judging yourself for having it, just observe it from a distance.

When you learn to separate yourself from thoughts as they come into your head, they have less power. You realise instead of them being all-encompassing terrors that you need to give all your mental energy to, they are really just an idea your brain decided you should consider. Therefore you can just not consider it, and your mind can be at peace.

If we approach our thoughts with an open and curious attitude, we can train our minds not to just fall into traps of worrying, self-criticising, or bringing up that random thing that makes you feel bad that you haven't thought about all day. Yes that thing. No – don't focus on it. Notice it, and now let it go. When you are fully detached from your thoughts and focused on the present moment, it's almost impossible to be anxious for the future or depressed about the past!

I am a self-confessed extreme ruminator. I can happily just sit in a loop fixated on something unresolved, or something I'm scared of, and let it dominate my day – remembering mindfulness and distancing myself from these thoughts is something I have to do roughly every three minutes, but at least I now know how.

Mindfulness is definitely a skill and for some people (hi) it takes practice. When I first started trying, it was very difficult to notice a thought without immediately jumping down the drain, instead of distancing myself from it. If that's you too, know that it's perfectly fine and expected. I won't always say you're perfectly fine if you're like me, but this time it's okay.

And for the fidgeters among us – it isn't about meditating for hours. Just remembering it when you notice a troubling thought, or trying to stay mindful for a few minutes while doing an activity, will help if you need it. As with breathing and being present, being mindful is something you can do at any time. You can even incorporate 'being mindful' into your day while doing physical tasks. I personally love doing a mindful dishwasher, folding the mindful laundry, or feeding the mindful highly diseased London pigeons.

EXERCISE: 1-MINUTE MINDFULNESS

Good for:
- **Centering yourself in the present moment**
- **Calming a busy mind**
- **Relaxing**

Focus on your breathing.

Whenever your mind wanders, or a thought pops up in your head, just acknowledge it and without judging or indulging the thought, gently bring attention back to your breathing. Do this for as long as you like, until you feel relaxed and calm.

That's it! The basic principle of mindfulness. Easy, right? And to think we were doing all that worrying when we could have let it float by like a cloud, a cloud shaped like that unread message I suddenly remembered while watering a plant, that must be critically important because my brain put it at the front of the queue. Thanks, mind.

The three tools of breathing, being present, and mindfulness, are incredibly powerful and allow you to instantly change how you feel – we will return to them throughout the book. Make sure you understand and practice them and you will be qualified to be a first-responder to what goes on in your head.

BREAKING IT DOWN

Our minds tend to just keep the thoughts rolling in as soon as we can conceive of something new to worry about, without asking first if we're comfortable with the information we've already been given. It's typical for a giant tangled ball of stress to formulate in the front of our minds, that at first feels like you've been thrown into unmanageable chaos – but if you interrupt the storm and break it down, you may realise there was a lot less to worry about than you thought.

The anxiety equation

Our anxiety is influenced by our thoughts. The way we think about something impacts how we feel about it. If you're feeling overwhelmed by something specific, try re-evaluating your thinking. One way to do this is called 'the anxiety equation'.

Sorry to all the math-phobes, as I learned when I studied Psychology in college, anything vaguely scientific will sooner or later involve statistics and formulae. Don't panic, I'm sensitive to my past self and any of you that relate to that, but I had to let one slip through. Plus this is a genuinely very helpful technique. I promise.

$$\text{ANXIETY ABOUT AN OUTCOME} = \frac{\text{LIKELIHOOD} \times \text{AWFULNESS}}{\text{COPING} + \text{RESCUE}}$$

In other words, how worried you are about something potentially happening is based on:

1. How likely you think it is to happen, combined with:
2. How awful you imagine it would be if it did happen.

This is reduced by:

3. How well you expect you'd cope with it if it did happen.
4. And how you think other people will respond.

Sounds simple like that, right? Not so much when I was quaking the other day, as I thought I had invoked the wrath of a neighbour by moving their recycling bags to the correct collection spot. They glared at me as though I was plotting to steal their used cardboard, which I immediately imagined would result in me being physically confronted and perhaps shunned by my entire neighbourhood – that is, before I broke the situation down and realised it was, really, fine. Not an international war crime.

What you may have noticed is this is all about how you perceive it. As we discussed before, how you feel about something may not necessarily be the truth, so breaking it down can make you instantly realise it's less intimidating than you thought, and actually – you can cope. Identify the thing that you're afraid of happening, then go through each question:

How likely is it that this will happen?

Forget how bad you feel about the idea of it, just think: in reality, what are the chances? When you buy a lottery ticket and feel like you 'know' it's your lucky day – that's called *emotional reasoning*. The feelings are so powerful, we actually believe in them, but just because you want to believe you will win the lottery, doesn't mean you're going to. Get real, Sandra.

How awful would it be if this thing happened?

My favourite pastime – 'catastrophising'. It is very human to imagine the worst-case scenario and fixate on what a compelling nightmarish story that would be. Even if the outcome is quite likely, if you really think about it and it's not actually that bad, you'll be fine.

It is very human
to imagine the
worst-case scenario.

Try to think what advice you'd give to someone else in your situation? How long would the outcome last? How long would they even be upset for, really? We love to indulge in imagining our own doom, even if we know it's nonsense and not how we'd help someone else. You'll probably be fine!

How well would I be able to cope?
When feeling anxious, it's easy to underestimate our resilience. Think about other difficulties you've faced in life – you probably survived all of those! Did you give yourself credit for that? If you can *imagine* a time in the future where you've managed to cope with whatever's in front of you now, you probably will.

What support can you get?
You are not alone in the universe, so who could be there for you for advice or consolation? Even if what you fear happens, the reality is other people are all far too obsessed with what's going on in their lives, so people won't think about you negatively nearly as much as you think they might.

The day I shared that I had struggled with depression, I went through this same cycle and felt prepared for any potentially bad outcomes, and even then I ended up surprised by the kindness and acceptance that I was met with. So don't beat yourself up. Who knows, you may actually win that metaphorical lottery!

The more you break it down, the calmer you will feel, and it will feel easier to resolve.

Workout plan

Say you've broken down your problem and it's less intimidating, sometimes you may still need help working out what to do. On a good day, most of us can handle problems and overcome things by thinking them through. On a bad day, month, or mental health downhill slide, we can be too occupied by negative thoughts and feelings swirling around our head, making us much less efficient. This is when it can help to be super-obvious, and literally remind ourselves how to think.

There are ways to make things easier. Be methodical. Be realistic.

THE CONTROLLER

The single most profound philosophy I apply in my day-to-day life is to separate what is within my control and what isn't. Any time spent worrying about something you can't change is a waste of time and energy that will just make you worse at doing the things you can. I know the thing may be annoying, or worrying (and compelling to sit dwelling on), but if you can't do something about it now – just let it go and move on. Then you can focus on what you can control, and you'll be more likely to succeed.

This is something I mastered through adversity when I was younger – and to give myself one single piece of kudos ever, it is honestly a superpower, which I credit for my super-resilience and victories against all the challenges of my life so far. If I had a dollar for every time I've watched friends stress and spiral over the infinite hypotheticals of a problem without solving the first step – I'd be Sandra who won the lottery. Bloody Sandra.

Don't let your mind lead you down the path of: 'but if this happens, then this happens, then what if this, then what if that, then how would I do that, then how would I ever manage this – guess I'm doomed.'

If your worry is 'my house just exploded and I'm about to host a birthday party' the worry is real and you should do something about it. If it's a 'what if', like 'what if my friend has a car accident and ruins their own birthday' then it's hypothetical; don't waste your time and energy thinking about it.

For **current worries**, tangible things, there is generally something you can do. Depending on your mental health you may need help in the problem-solving department, so remember to break it down, take it step by step, ask for help and share that you are struggling.

For **hypothetical worries**, there is not usually much you can do, because right now it isn't real. The best thing to do in this situation is to let go. By moving on you are free to focus on what is in front of you without wasting your time. After all, you can always worry about it later if it suddenly becomes real – I'm basically giving you a free pass to procrastinate. Enjoy it.

No matter what problem pops up in the path of your life, from rescuing a drowning bee, to piloting a flaming escape-pod that you somehow ended up responsible for during the first manned mission to Jupiter – take it one step at a time and only dedicate your brain energy to working on things you can actually change.

Remember mindfulness – letting go of your hypothetical worries doesn't mean pushing them out of your head or being in denial. Acknowledge and appreciate them, just don't focus on them if they don't help. Focus on what you're achieving in the present.

Thought suppression is the technical term for suppressing what's on your mind, and there's lots of evidence to show that it just makes the negative thoughts stronger. For example: right now, think of the last person you saw. Next, *do not* imagine that person completely naked. Boom. Depending on who you may have had the misfortune of meeting previously, I may have potentially just ruined your entire day, because you're definitely imagining it right now. This is the paradoxical effect of just trying to ignore something on your mind. It's still there. (It's still there – and totally nude.)

It's also worth knowing that most of the things humans worry about don't actually happen. Research has shown that people worry about a lot of things in a day, and the majority of them never occur. Even when they do, people usually cope much better than they expected. So what are you worrying for? What a waste of time!

EXERCISE: LETTING GO OF WORRIES

Good for:
- **Stopping circular thoughts**
- **Freeing your mind**
- **Tackling anxiety**

Take the thing you are worried about. Think about what you're experiencing – what are you thinking about it, how do you feel emotionally, how do you feel physically?

Determine if the worry is something you can change.

If it's **current**, plan to problem-solve it. Clearly define what the issue is. Break it down into smaller parts and think of solutions. Evaluate all your options, work out what can be done now, and what needs to wait until later. Get help if you need it, action the steps that you can, decide how to deal with the rest, then review how it all went and see what's left to solve.

If it's **hypothetical**, simply observe the worrying thought. Don't try to change it, just realise it's there, and then aim to let it go when you can. Remind yourself that you can come back to it later if it does become a tangible problem.

If you're still feeling anxious and struggle to let go of the worry, gently bring your focus to your breathing and the physical world around you. Don't fight the feelings, let them drift by until you feel in a more calm place.

Need to talk?

Out of any technique, one of the most powerful ways to intervene and manage your mental health is to talk to someone. I say this as an extreme introvert, who literally does not enjoy talking to people (even with close friends on a quiet day, never mind strangers), but I have learned through my struggles that when you are feeling low, feeling that connection – the sensation that you are not alone, that you are being acknowledged and listened to – can be a tether to reality and a literal lifeline. I wouldn't be here today if it weren't for doctors, therapists and friends, and I am thankful for them every day.

Depending on how badly you feel, you may want to talk to someone right away, or when you're ready.

If you want to talk to someone in your life, think of who you can turn to, who you can trust. It's easy to tell ourselves that other people won't want to hear us complain, or will judge us for admitting we feel bad, but it's a fact that most people would rather listen than know you were suffering in silence. I'm sure we've all had moments when someone we're close to shared something with us, and we were surprised and saddened that they'd been carrying the burden for so long. You and I are just the same. Remember, mental health problems are something we all have, so it may seem hard to start the conversation, but remember that it's normal and relatable. It may even bring you closer to and help the ones you reach out to!

If you feel there's nobody around you that you can talk to right now, that's okay, hopefully there are professionals you can turn to. Depending on what you can access in your circumstances (such as geographic, cultural or even financial constraints), you could see a doctor, a therapist or counsellor, call a free helpline or even an online chat – any human connection will count for something. You don't have to be in a crisis before you contact them, you can even reach out to practice or just establish a connection. Professionals are trained to treat you with respect and non-judgement, and they will have heard it all so they won't be shocked by what you say. Most importantly, professionals are committed to confidentiality – if you're in doubt, just ask them.

Whoever you decide to talk to, think about what you want to say and how much you want to share. It's your story, you are in control of how much you share – even if it's simply that you need help. It's a start.

IN CASE OF EMERGENCY

Sometimes in life, things overwhelm us to a breaking point, or a slow burn of suffering pushes us to an edge we don't think we can recover from. If you ever think you're in danger of hurting yourself or others, the best thing is to connect with another person. Talking to another person can ground you, put things into perspective, and give you hope. If anything, it can distract you until you get out of a destructive headspace which may totally change how you feel. You could reach out to someone you trust, call a helpline or in an emergency go to your nearest hospital. Even if you don't feel like talking, or are afraid to, if you know you're feeling this way, just go to a place you feel safe in the presence of others.

You may not think your doctor would be the person for mental health problems, but they can be the best! A doctor can assess you personally, make a diagnosis, and refer you forward to any specialists. Try to be as descriptive and honest as possible – it's understandable to feel nervous, so you could prepare what to say before, write it down or even bring someone along for support. The most important thing is that you go.

Never make big decisions in a heightened emotional state, and remember that no matter what is happening in your life, the feeling is temporary. There is always something that every single one of us can do, whether that's tomorrow (when we have a plan), or just with the passage of time. Circumstances always change – so don't do anything that you can't change.

Breakdowns
can be
breakthroughs.

Good night

Tomorrow is a new day. Whether it's literally one night, or some hard times, if you can make it through you will get another chance to try again.

Even if you haven't managed to win yet, think about one thing you could try tomorrow to take you one step closer to feeling better. Maybe it's just finding a moment to take a breath, try to feel present, or practice mindfulness. Don't put pressure on yourself, but feel reassured that now you know there are things you can do to make yourself feel better. Each sunrise brings the chance to start afresh, feeling re-energised, with the opportunity to make a change.

The cliché is that night is darkest just before the dawn, but it's often in these moments of confrontation and reflection that we learn something. Sometimes, periods of feeling bad and uncertainty can push us through to finally understanding or acknowledging something – breakdowns can be breakthroughs. We spend so much of our lives running away from problems, that if the dam bursts in a dramatic moment, it can be the truth finally setting itself free. It may be upsetting to snap, but the good news is: if you feel like you've hit the bottom, the only way is up. I can tell you that at so many times in my life when I felt I couldn't see the light, there was always a way. Whether I lifted myself, was carried by the people around me, or the passage of time changed my point of view – there's always tomorrow.

Part 2

TOMORROW

TOMORROW

This part is for when you're in a place where you can make some small changes, that in a few days should help your mind so you have fewer difficult nights. There are certain things we all can do, things within our control, to make the best of the situation we're in. Once you're in the right headspace, then you'll be in a place to think about the bigger things.

This part is about laying the foundations for positive momentum, because if you're like me and need all the help you can get, why not help yourself? We'll go through different areas of life that have been proven to affect your mental health. You can decide what makes sense for your circumstances and what works for you – you may be doing some of this already, or none of it – and give it all a shot. Hey, if it turns out you're already doing it all, congrats! Go forth and thrive in it. Otherwise, get cracking.

YOU ARE NOT GOD (SORRY)

A fact of life I personally refuse to come to terms with is that you cannot control everything. Part of my classic complex is that as a result of my chaotic childhood, I demand perfection and total control over every aspect of my life. Everything must be optimised and the slightest inconvenience is a calamity. I live by the phrase 'if you want something doing right, do it yourself', and I also die by it, as it's exhausting and makes me resentful. Whilst I'm good at ignoring factors totally outside of my influence, if there's a sneaky chance I could intervene . . . I cannot let it go. I'm trying to be better at this.

No matter how it affects you or annoys you, you can't control other people, what's happening in the news, or the incoming inclement weather threatening to really emphasise your suffering as you walk outside in socks to recycle all the cardboard you've been hoarding for weeks. We all dedicate a lot of mental energy to worrying about and being annoyed by these things outside of our influence – but as we begin this part, I am officially giving you permission to take a break from this unhelpful habit. Let's give our attention and time to the things we can make better.

PRO-TIP (LITERALLY)

Remember, nothing here is intended to replace the advice of a professional. If you're seeing a therapist or any other specialist, they should have a good understanding of your personality and unique circumstances! You can always consult a professional on any idea in this book to see if it works for you, or if this book encourages you to reach out for help, that's great. It could be a trusted friend, qualified healthcare worker or a wise elderly person who appeared mysteriously on a bench, dispensing nuggets of profound wisdom.

CALM DOWN AND SLOW DOWN

As fun as it is to wake up one morning and decide to totally revolutionise your life, that's probably not a good idea. It's okay; I too fantasise about spontaneously moving country, deleting half my friends, getting a job as an apprentice pastry chef in an imaginarily undefined European city and magically living an unrealistic dream life where I have no worries . . . but maybe I just needed to open the curtains. No judgement here.

Take things step by step. You may wonder how a dozen tiny changes can really change how you feel, but allow yourself to take it slow, and feel proud of yourself if you try just one thing to improve your day-to-day life. It also helps to focus on what you can do right now, rather than what you think you 'should do' and becoming that unhelpful all-consuming ball of anxiety.

Burnout is a real thing and, especially if you've been feeling low, I appreciate the desire to get going to turn your life around – just don't do it at 1,000 mph, and when one tiny thing goes wrong erupt into a ball of flames, and have an even more spectacular meltdown than whatever prompted your self-improvement moment in the first place. Take your time, set achievable goals, be proud of any progress... and calm down.

THE FIVE MINUTE RULE

This isn't about how long food can be on the floor before you eat it, you're disgusting. This is a real motivation masterclass. We often tell ourselves that we 'don't have the energy' or motivation to do something, but usually motivation kicks in after we start, not before, so it's about encouraging the very first step. As the top ranked worst-procrastinator-in-the-entire-world, I'm qualified to say: putting something off hoping you will 'feel motivated' later usually means you will never start. Sometimes when we take just the tiniest first step, it's suddenly not so intimidating.

One small step for you . . . will probably be one giant leap for you.

I can be classified as a procrastinating perfectionist. Or the world's slowest workaholic. This may sound oxymoronic (or just moronic) but you may just need to reframe how you see procrastination. I used to think that my procrastination meant I didn't want to work, but do something fun instead. That didn't make sense, however, as now I choose what work I do as I'm passionate about it, and when I get stuck into anything I do, I enthusiastically overwork to complete self-destruction. Procrastination is about fear. Fear that the task ahead of you will be difficult, that it will be overwhelming, that you might fail. If I sat aimlessly refreshing the same two apps on my phone for two hours, procrastinating as my 'fun alternative' to that thing I don't want to do, I'm not actually having fun myself, I'm just prolonging my suffering as I sit there totally failing to enjoy my procrastination activity, feeling terrible the whole time. If you are a total procrastinator, it doesn't mean you're a bad person. In fact, it probably means you care more about what you have to do than the average person, because you don't want to half-ass it. I always want everything to be perfect, which is why I'm so slow to start anything I work on, because it's terrifying – and here is where the five minute rule comes in.

Simply commit to doing something for five minutes. Five minutes and you are allowed to stop. Set a timer, even. Get stuck in and I bet that when that five minutes is up, you will magically find yourself willing to keep going. It turns out that thing wasn't the horrifying nightmare you were afraid of, you were just afraid to start. It's comparable to trying to keep your mind 'in the present' as opposed to hypothetical worries about the future.

I didn't write this book in five minutes, but you bet your butt that once I started I somehow found myself typing five hours later. Even if your task is huge and long and painful, say to yourself that you will do the most ridiculously inconsequential amount of work on it, just the tip, and you may find that you accidentally tackled the whole thing. If not, then that's okay. After all, you gave yourself permission to stop.

Simply commit to
doing something for
five minutes.
Five minutes and you
are allowed to stop.

ACTIVITY

There's a link between what we do and how we feel, and this works both ways: the way we feel influences what we do, and what we do directly impacts how we feel.

When we're feeling down, it's easy to think there's nothing we can do about it. Sometimes there are things beyond our control – but we can always choose to do things that help our mood.

The feedback loop

Our brains have a default habit that is either kind of helpful or complete sabotage. When we feel good, we want to do things that make us feel good, like achieving goals that feel rewarding, being creative, doing exercise, etc. Without realising it, a positive mood makes us want to continue positive momentum.

The same is true of the opposite. When we feel bad we tend to want to do the kind of things that ultimately make us feel worse. If we're stressed and tired, we won't want to work – then we feel bad. Or we put off having a shower or doing laundry – then later we feel bad. When we're in this negative mood it snowballs down until life feels like an unstoppable avalanche. This is when we tell ourselves we're bad, or not good enough. It can lead to other outcomes, where people criticise you, or you have to compromise on what you want. Before we know it, we're trapped in a vicious cycle where we feel bad, so we do less, so we feel worse – but we can choose to turn this around.

Take a moment to think about what you've been doing lately. Do you feel like you're on a roll, or are things a struggle? Are you managing the basics like eating, sleeping and doing work? Are you taking time to do things you enjoy? Or maybe these things are taking too much energy and you feel you don't have the time or space? Maybe there are some unhelpful habits you know you've been doing more of?

If you catch yourself in this cycle, it's not because you're a failure, you're just in the zone where the negative spiral takes over. Think of it like your low mood is making these decisions for you, rather than something you chose.

Positive propulsion

The upside is that planning positive activity can lift your mood and put you on the right track. We don't need to wait to magically feel better, or for something out of our control to turn fortunate, we can kick-start our mood whenever we want.

In times of my life when I've struggled with depression – sometimes a day, sometimes weeks at a time – I used to say there were 'bad days', when I just had to accept that my mental health was so bad I wouldn't be good for anything. But whilst it's important to be fair to yourself and take time if you need it, I was wrong that I had to just accept how I felt and deal with it, lying face-down on the floor, neck-deep in a pile of beige snacks and blankets.

If we understand the links between our thoughts, how those thoughts make us feel, and how our feelings influence what we do – we can choose to do something that makes us feel more positive. Whether or not you ever feel depressed, this principle applies to everything, and is something to always remember. You've got the power.

Three kinds of activity are:

ROUTINE ACTIVITIES

Part of your daily routine. Basic self-care and life maintenance.
Eating, showering, brushing your teeth. Important for functioning
as a human and fundamental for feeling good.

NECESSARY ACTIVITIES

These are the things you have to do. Going to work or class,
finishing projects, paying the bills. If you don't do these, there
are probably negative consequences – but when you do do them,
you have a sense of accomplishment and purpose. My purpose
is to feel resentful as I pay the bills. I know unlimited internet
is necessary for my lifestyle, but I reserve the right to complain
about how expensive it is.

PLEASURE ACTIVITIES

No, not just that, go to horny jail *bonk*. This is anything
you enjoy. If you focus all your time and energy on the basics
and obligations, life will feel pretty dull. So yes, it is literally,
scientifically, psychologically, profoundly important to have fun.
The hard part is the balance.

Prioritisation (A.K.A. professional procrastination)

I don't think it's controversial to assume that you, like me, rarely feel like you are on top of absolutely everything in your life and have nothing to do ahead of you. If I'm wrong, throw this book at the first person you think needs it.

The trouble, when you want to start turning things around, is prioritising the order of everything in your life – but time is money. Or should we say, money is your metaphorical mood, and the time it takes to make your mood good should be as short as possible, so it's time to get rich quick . . . emotionally.

STEP 1:
THINK OF ALL THE THINGS YOU NEED TO DO

Are you barely being a human? It might sound obvious, but in an incredibly anxious afternoon, stressful series of days, or deep cave of depression, you might have forgotten to sleep enough, eat any time recently, or have a bath – you stinky mutt.

What tasks do you need to get done? List all the things that are on your mind, literally hovering over your mood, putting the pressure on.

What might you enjoy? Is there something you've been excited to do? A fun activity you're looking for an excuse to approve?! Yes, there's a glimmer of hope. Hold on to these things.

STEP 2:
PRIORITISE THE THINGS

How much effort is this thing to do? How much better will doing it make you feel?

Go through each thing, deciding whether they are low effort or high effort – and low value or high value. This should show you what activities may be really easy to do, and also make you feel better (like eating) or incredibly difficult and not that beneficial (like rearranging your entire wardrobe from light to dark, which I may or may not have done recently for no apparent reason or benefit).

Then if you want to feel better, do the things you need to do in the most efficient order for your mood!

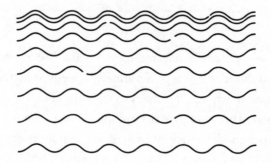

	HIGH VALUE	LOW VALUE
LOW EFFORT	**Do it** • Showering • Drinking some water • Texting concerned relative back • Remembering to charge your imminently dead phone	**Save for later** • Dabbing • Biting your fingernails • Flipping toilet roll to face the *correct* way on the holder • Adjusting your hair in the mirror for an hour
HIGH EFFORT	**Plan for later** • Rewriting CV • Filling in tax return • Visiting a concerned relative • Writing a 320 page book	**These can wait** • Trying to open a coconut • Taking all the curtains down and cleaning them • Re-organising bookshelf according to colour • Renaming and sorting files in your meme folder

This is more technically referred to as a 'value / effort matrix', but I like to think of it as a professionally approved method of procrastination, where I feel like I'm cheating, but it makes me feel good. Turns out procrastination is one of those social standards our modern society created just to put pressure on and make us feel bad constantly, for no good reason, when there's something we could have done about it the whole time.

Prioritising things in order of effort, and their value to you, gives you a maximum mood boost for your time, and is a sure-fire way to improve your mental state and feel in control.

Low effort, high value tasks are what you can do in that state of procrastination paralysation, or when everything feels like a struggle. They will make you feel accomplished, but can be managed on autopilot if you're having 'one of those mental health days'. No one will accuse you of cheating for taking these easy wins – enjoy it.

High effort, high value tasks are things that are important, but clearly require more planning and thought. So rather than imagining the horror now and sweating under the spotlight as you drain the day away in dread, perhaps just start planning them and allow yourself to cross some other things off your list first. Separate what you can realistically do now from what you can only do later, and focus on the now. When you get around to tackling the terror-task, break it down, try five minutes, be patient with yourself, and remember that as catastrophic as your brain may be trying to convince you this challenge is, it is not *actually* a giant meteor threatening to crash from space and eradicate your entire existence.

If it's low value, high effort – let it go until you're ready.

Disclaimer: I'm not personally responsible if you categorised 'putting out that fire in my room right now' in this category, and procrastinated. It's on you to use the matrix responsibly.

Excuse the excuses

When it's time to get stuff done, people are very good at inventing reasons to struggle, and struggling to start. If our mental health is good, we will naturally be better planners and prioritisers; if we're going through a down-time, we might feel overwhelmed and need to be reminded of the basics. I don't want to personally attack your intelligence with the following potentially extremely fundamental information, so let's frame it like I'm talking to myself, at the times when I know I definitely needed to hear all of this.

Know yourself – be honest about who you know you are. If you get out of bed at 10 a.m., don't act like you can magically wake up at dawn merrily whistling with the wildlife, because you'll collapse an hour later and the rest of the day will be a write-off. Do low effort things when you know you're low energy, do the high effort things when you know you're available and awake.

Commit to it – we're more likely to do things when we commit and hold ourselves accountable. Rather than specifically feeling like you'll do 'all the things', say to yourself you will do that one thing that is important.

Make it real – write it down. Put it in your planner. Be pedantic with yourself. Plan every hour of your day, every microsecond of the process. Make plans with other people to make sure you turn up, and hold you accountable. Remind yourself what you're doing, when you're doing it and most importantly why you're doing it and how it will help you. I tend to enter a situation I committed to months ago with murderous rage at my past self, having completely forgotten the importance of whatever the task is – help yourself remember.

Finally: have fun – if you don't eventually prioritise enjoying your life, you will definitely and measurably be worse at all the other less enjoyable stuff you may be telling yourself you have to do instead of having fun. This is basic self-care and also a good check to see how fairly you are treating yourself – it's perfectly reasonable to take a moment to go outside or listen to music. If you're telling yourself, 'no you horrible ugly disgusting swamp creature go back to your mandatory tasks you grovelling idiot how dare you be so indulgent you make me sick,' then you're not being reasonable, or right. Rest has been proven to be critical for good performance and learning. Doing things we enjoy is a good emotional and energy reset too – you could work all weekend, but if you allow yourself an evening to do something fun you may find you're more focused and productive the next day. Commit to the fun.

I'm a notorious over-committer to projects, who loves imposing a looming deadline as motivation (as nothing personally gets me moving like guilt and shame). My go-to strategy is riding the line where my life may collapse into complete unmitigated disaster if I don't do something, so I need to constantly remind myself that if I just try five minutes I'll probably do it, and I don't have to wait until the very last minute where I crunch everything in a caffeine-fuelled craze. I started one piece of coursework for Law School at 3 a.m. on the day it was due. Never again.

The thought police

As we discussed earlier, one of the most important things to remember is that you are not your thoughts. Your thoughts are driven by impulses, influenced by how you feel and what you do, shaped by your experiences in life. It's not surprising that if we try to do something we don't want to, our thoughts may pop up with unhelpful suggestions like:

- 'I will not enjoy this.'

- 'I will be bad at this.'

- 'I don't have the energy for this.'

- 'I don't deserve to do this.'

- 'What if I projectile vomit?'

- 'What is the point?'

Indulging these kinds of thoughts can be toxic and totally obstruct your ability to succeed at what you're doing. This is the time to make your mind 'mindful'. When the thought comes in, notice it, then try to question it. Where did that thought come from? What are you afraid of? Is it real, or if you stick to the plan will it be fine? If you can't rationalise it and it's hard to ignore, remember that it's just a thought in your head and try to let it go.

Getting to know yourself

Most of us cruise through life not analysing every single thing we do, why we do it, and how it makes us feel – because we're not weird. However, if we do start to pay attention to the relationship between what we do and how we feel, we can go ahead in life with a plan we know works.

If you think about your last week, what was the best day and worst day? What were you feeling and what were you doing?

Humans are prone to another unhelpful behaviour called *mood congruence* – which means when we feel low we remember and emphasise the other times we feel low, and when we feel good we tend to connect positive memories and have a rosier view on life. So when you thought about last week, your brain probably went fishing for a time where you felt similar to how you do now? If this was like a shocking mind-reading mentalism moment for you and you think I'm psychic – I don't know if that either makes stage magic suddenly underwhelming, or makes basic behavioural science seem impressive. Turns out we're not that complicated, but we do come with a bunch of unhelpful programming that I'd ideally remove with a brain virus scan.

I personally lose scope of my feelings too often. If I'm having a great day, I feel generally optimistic and struggle to relate to that recent time I felt total doom and gloom. On a bad day, I struggle to find hope or meaning in anything. The truth is, depending on our mental health programming and the world around us, our moods vary constantly. Which is why taking notice, noting and trying to remember this can be such a helpful perspective.

If you want to write it out, pick a day and write the time, how you feel, and what you are doing. It's important to understand that you're never doing *nothing*. Even if you spent the afternoon in a state of constant light-nap, watching videos of family dogs being introduced to babies for the first time, that is a valid and notable activity. It will make you feel something. Probably very ugly tears. Write that shit down. How do you feel?

DAY / TIME	ACTIVITY	MOOD OUT OF 10
Sunday 11am	Trying to find the edge of a piece of tape	2
Sunday 3pm	Dog videos and eating ice cream	Emotionally raw but a 9??
Sunday 4pm	Brain-freeze induced migraine	3

Seeing the science

Try this for a few days, or a week, and then stand back and look at all the data you generated. You did it, you did a science. You can see what activities make your mood better or worse – and you may find some surprises. You could notice some correlations you wouldn't have picked up on before, like thinking you 'hate exercise' but after going for a run you always felt 8/10.

For me, I've realised that if I look at the news in the evening, I feel worse and get more stressed than if I do it in the morning (when I have the energy and resilience to absorb the latest horrors of the universe). It was also profoundly beneficial for me to know that playing certain competitive shooter games, that I consider fun, seems to consistently make me angry in the middle of an otherwise tolerable afternoon. Some things just aren't good for my blood pressure.

It can also be good just to see how you feel if/when you finally get around to those routine or necessary tasks you've been putting off. If it turns out you consistently feel better after your chores, as you feel purpose and accomplishment, knowing you will feel good afterwards may help put off the procrastination poltergeist that's holding you back.

With this objective view of who you really are, and how you work (not just how we *like* to think we work and understand ourselves, which is probably more forgiving than reality), you can plan your life and the tasks you need to do around the things and time you know will work best for you and put you in the best mood. Sure, it's easy to tackle life on autopilot, but if you ever start feeling like things could be easier, or you just don't have the momentum or energy to think about how to improve your life, this is a head start to give yourself a boost.

You feel what you do. You control what you do. You can have some control over how you feel.

ACTIVITY CHEAT SHEET

- What you do affects how you feel.

- Procrastination is fear and sometimes just starting is the solution.

- Break down what you have to do into: routine / necessary / pleasure.

- Work out what is worth the effort and value.

- Prioritise and be practical.

- Don't let your thoughts get in the way.

- Celebrate the wins and be fair to yourself.

- Make a note of what you did and how you feel.

- Learn from this and go forward knowing how you work!

You feel what you do.

You control what you do.

You can have some control over how you feel.

ENVIRONMENT

The world around us affects our mental health just as much as what happens in our minds. We should do everything we can to make our environment the best space to live in, physically and mentally.

Creating a safe and comfortable environment to retreat back to is the base that can support you through hard times and any changes you want to make in life. Ask what you can do to make your surroundings improve your mental health, rather than cause stress!

Home is where the mind is

Humans are used to having a place to return to, to feel safe and secure – while that may not be true for your home, it's what it should be. We all deserve to have a place that makes us feel safe, physically and psychologically. Making just a few small changes in your space can set the ball rolling for progress everywhere else.

Your space may be a mansion, a maisonette, a single bedroom, or even just a bed in a shared space – what's important is what we have control over. Don't fret about the parts you can't influence, and focus on what you can change. Even if your space is temporary, it's important to put your mark on it so you feel like you belong. I lived in a student dormitory room in Manchester that looked like some kind of dank medieval dungeon cell, with a mysteriously stained second-hand mattress – but you better believe I asserted dominance over that oppressive environment by sticking posters all over the walls and holding back the darkness with a bright blue lava lamp. It was *my* dank medieval dungeon cell.

TIDY ROOM, TIDY MIND

This is the truth that my teenage self was simply not ready to hear or accept. If your environment is cluttered, it can make you stressed. I know, really, I *know* that the pile of clothes in the corner – that may be home to a small colony of feral rodents – seems like an unclimbable literal mountain of labour, that you can technically squeeze around to enter and leave the room. But if you just do the laundry you will feel better.

A pile of dishes isn't just a biohazard waiting to happen, it's a constant nag on your mind that will add a looming presence of guilt that won't help everything else you have going on. The chaotic desk will make your work harder. Removing constant reminders of tasks you 'should have done' will give you the physical space and mental clarity to take on life's challenges and think about the bigger things. If you feel overwhelmed, just make a start. Try five minutes. If you're just feeling lazy… get off your ass because you'll probably feel better afterwards. Just don't go overboard – some people try to overcompensate small tasks as a form of procrastinating the bigger things, and decide to completely renovate their homes and pull out every drawer, only to have a complete breakdown halfway through, and they've actually just made it worse. To start, just do the laundry, leave your aspiring interior decorator daydream for later.

For some reading this, it may be painfully obvious – and perhaps even childish – to be reminded to tidy, but do appreciate that, firstly, some people are just chaotic messy individuals who may be more stressed than they need to be (if this is you – yes this is a personal attack), but also, anyone going through a mental health problem may be really struggling with the basics and not know where to start. In periods of my life when I felt overly stressed or stuck in a depression, my home became a reflection of my mental health, that got worse the deeper I fell. Sometimes letting the light in and inhaling the fresh air is the first literal step to lifting yourself out of the darkness.

LET THERE BE LIGHT

Humans are really just complicated plants. Sometimes I look at one of my mildly struggling succulents and wonder if I could trade places – cacti don't get stressed, right? We need air and light to live. Natural light controls the circadian rhythms that dictate our sleep and energy cycles. The quality of the air we breathe affects how clearly our brain can operate, and our long-term health. Depending on what you can achieve, try to let in as much daylight in as possible and let air circulate. If you don't have a lot of light, use mirrors. If your schedule or location on earth means you don't see a lot of daylight (or are just an insomniac nerd like me) getting a 'light box' lamp, often used to treat 'Seasonal Affective Disorder' in the winter, can be an amazing help. Do what you can.

GO GREEN

As a proud plant dad, I can advocate for the power of caring for some cacti – plants in your environment can boost your mental wellbeing! They make your air fresher, your space look nicer, and help your sense of purpose by caring for something else (the day my 'peace lily' flowered, I felt prouder than when I passed my driving test). They're usually inexpensive and pretty easy, so take the leap. Become a plant person. Just don't get emotionally attached to a bonsai you spontaneously buy and then instantly murder by overwatering . . . mentioning that for no specific reason.

Enjoy the view

Another thing to consider is how the objects you see in your space make you feel. Everything you see usually has some context behind it which causes a different 'mood trigger'. If you see something that makes you feel good, or gives you a good memory when you walk past it, it is a constant boost to your mental health. If something looks bad or triggers bad memories, you may not have appreciated this, but removing it from view can keep you feeling better more often. Now, I'm not saying to cover your room with uplifting quotes and motivational posters, unless you're into that (judgement and shame upon you), just look around your space and think about how the things around you make you feel. Put out photos of good times, things that make you laugh, or something that inspires you. Anything you can't decorate with, or find space for, you can always put in a box so you have a treasure chest of instant good vibes whenever you need to feel better.

It can be hard to recognise if objects we think 'should' be displayed and make us feel good actually make us feel worse. I had a lot of old photos that, when I thought about it, looking at made me feel regretful and reminded me of things I'd lost. Cues can be so subtle that they're completely beyond our conscious awareness – so if you side-eye something and get just a twinge of negativity, move it, chuck it, paint over it. It doesn't have to be permanent, but it makes things that little bit easier. People often ask why I don't have more personal photos or career achievements on display, and I reply that I don't want them on display, that what I have visible makes me feel good, and then I push them out of a window for being annoying.

Easy mode

'Easy Access Motivators' are things to have around you that make life easier. If you know you need certain things day-to-day: keys, phone, tape-measure, watering can, dumbbells, anime body pillow – make them easy to access. If you struggle to get up and go exercise, or you're always late as it takes an hour to pack your bag, lay out and pack your things the night before. Conversely, you can hide the things that aren't helpful, if you know that having certain objects lying around are a distraction, or lead you towards destructive behaviour. Take a moment when you have the time and the mental space, and you will thank yourself for being a telepathic genius when you most desperately need it. If you're already a well-functioning human reading this, this might just be a little optimisation. If you're in the midst of a mental health mire, because things have suddenly taken a dip, this might be the little advantage you prepared for yourself earlier, that gets you through a tough time.

Minimalism

This word means a lot, ironically, and it could be referring to a million different things. Without diving into a swamp of debate about everything from art to interior design, and the relationship between capitalism, materialism and any in-built human desires to hoard... sometimes there's stuff we don't need. If you have too much crap that you don't use or don't like, give some away. It's a bit simple to state that if you lived in an empty white cube with only a single concrete table, your mental health struggles would be magically 'cured'. You certainly don't need to buy expensive things that are supposedly 'minimal', or, conversely, feel bad if you can't afford to own many possessions at all – it's just about how what you have makes you feel.

There is an argument that removing the number of choices you have to make in a day can streamline your brain power to focus on what's important. Some tech-billionaire lizard-person who only wears the same T-shirt every single day? I mean, sure, that is an incredibly optimised way of life. If your brain is genuinely so full that choosing between black and grey socks will send you over the edge – go all in. For some people, though, it's the total opposite! You may walk into the most overstocked, grossly over-decorated room with so much stuff you will never touch and think 'ah, yes, home' and if that's you, you are valid. If your idea of peace is the reassuring presence of a million dusty books haphazardly piled around the place, then I'm happy for you. For most of us there's a sensible middle ground between not living in clutter, seeing things that make us feel good, making life easier for ourselves, and not feeling pressured to own too much or too little. Make your home *yours*.

MINDFUL MAINTENANCE

Remember that any activity is an opportunity to change how you feel, and even if fixing your environment feels like work, you can make it work for you. You can multitask with music or, as I do, walk around accomplishing everything at half speed because you're watching something on your phone in one hand the whole time – as long as it gets done.

It can also be a good time to practice mindfulness. If you need to feel calmer, enjoy the silence and focus. Take your time, be slow if necessary, and use tasks as a chance to be in the present. Focus on your senses, feel more tethered to the physical world than in your mind, and separate yourself from your thoughts.

Working from home

If you work or study at home, it can be hard to keep boundaries between the different parts of your life. For people who leave their home, there is a change of scenery and mindset. You can 'leave' certain feelings in that place and switch off. The ability to rest is so important, as typically we go through waves of high-stress, intense situations in our days, then need to slow right down to recover afterwards. This is why people who have a harmful home environment are so much more susceptible to mental health problems, as home may not provide a place to recover.

Speaking as a self-employed person, doing absolutely everything from your own place has its pros and cons. Sure, you may be able to sneak a few extra minutes in bed, but you're just as likely to feel obligated to work in the evenings, and feel a constant sense of pressure and guilt as there is no separation between work and rest. As times change with technology, or particular global incidents force people to stay inside for long periods of time *cough*, more of us may find ourselves having to work from home – so it's important to know how to keep balance.

Zoning – try to use different spaces for different activities. Some people have the privilege of a home office, but even if you do everything in one room you can treat a bed differently to a chair or the floor. The more separation between sleep, work and fun the better.

In the disturbing early days of my content-creating career, I did *everything* in one room – from sleeping, to filming, eating, editing and emailing, and woke up every morning confronted with the things that had been stressing me out in the day before. Years went by before I thought 'this is not ideal' and did something about it. Don't sleep with a camera pointed at your bed, for your mental health or your neighbours'. Don't be me.

Routine – if you have the option to spend all day in pyjamas, I don't blame you for trying it. I will not lie, it is how I live. I am very physically comfortable as I write this – however, it can be devastating for productivity, and make down time less meaningful. You have to make an extra effort to take that shower in the morning, put on a set of 'day clothes' and 'begin' your tasks to switch your mindset into productivity, or the day will just sink into the sofa you find yourself hopelessly embedded in.

Schedule – commit yourself to when you will begin and end the tasks you need to do. Defining these things can solidify them in your mind, compelling you to start and giving you permission to switch off. We need breaks, not just to sustain productivity, or, y'know, eat and maintain other bodily functions, so remember to schedule and take breaks. Finally – at the end of the work day put away any objects that will remind you of your job, or keep you working. I have friends who don't turn off their work notifications in the evenings, pinging and dinging every other minute, completely obliterating the mood. If you're reading this book, please. I'm begging you. I don't want to be reminded of that thing I haven't responded to yet.

Negotiations – if you're with others, you might need to discuss how things work. Do you need space, quiet, concentration, or for someone not to use all the internet bandwidth while you have an important video meeting looking like a Tamagotchi? Probably the most difficult aspect of your environment to improve, for your mental health, are the people you share it with.

More people, more problems

Most of us live, by choice (or circumstance) with friends, partners, parents or strange housemates. And what these people are like obviously influences the state of our home environments and mental health in general. There needs to be a mutual understanding and appreciation of boundaries, how long people can use communal areas, how long is too long to hog the damn shower, and however the hell you work out who controls the TV.

These relationships change over time. Whatever happens to someone outside the home, they bring back into the home. It might not be your fault, but if you live together it will affect you. People come and go. Power dynamics come into play if one person owns the property (or does more than their fair share of work) and when circumstances change things can get turbulent. Resentments bubble over time into something bigger, which is why being open about things, and having agreed ground rules, makes life at home more stable. Of course, some people, particularly the young, are not in a position to question or change the people they live with, in which case they may have to tolerate a toxic situation until they can find an alternative – what's important is that we recognize and don't accept situations that are bad for our mental health.

I remember being sixteen and trying to hatch a plan where I could move to the big city and instantly start my new independent life on my terms. The plan made literally no sense and would never have worked in a million years, but time passes, circumstances change, and before I knew it I was living in London paying more in rent than I earned in a year. Finally, I was free?

SCENE CHANGE

If you're in a negative headspace, having a change of scene can be really helpful. Particularly if you've had a bad night and don't feel better the next morning, getting away from the place and everything associated with it can help clear your head and reset. Go for a walk, enjoy a drink, meet up with a friend – try to focus on whatever you're doing in this new location, instead of dwelling on the negative thoughts you're trying to step away from. Then when you return to your place, you will have a fresh perspective and a different energy.

The (not so?) great outdoors

Your 'environment' is more than just the space you live in – it's also where you spend your time. The places you regularly travel, work, socialise. It's good to think about the difference between the places we *have* to spend time and where we choose to.

Of all the places you tend to go, where do you feel happiest? Most relaxed or confident? Consider what it is about these places that makes you feel good. Can you spend more time there, or in other places that will make you feel the same way? Also, try to think about places that make you feel down. We may not realise it, but perhaps somewhere we spend a lot of time in our routine has negative associations – can you change anything here? Spend less time there? We can learn a lot about ourselves by questioning why places make us feel differently, and choosing to follow the things that are good for us!

FOREST BATHING

Not having a bath in the forest – that sounds kind of scary to me? What if you get sniffed out by some wolves? Hopefully you can still streak fast while covered in bubbles.

In Japan, there is the concept of *shinrin yoku* (forest bathing), which simply means going into the woods and letting your senses get washed over by nature. You don't have to be in dense wilderness; even a small public park, or some plants in a tiny outside space, can take you out of your mind and ground you to the physical world. Interacting with plants can even calm us by steadying our heart rate, and reduce negative feelings like anxiety and depression.

Fresh air and natural light are good for us, but there are psychological benefits to even just looking at pictures of nature. Colours, on a basic level, can influence our emotions. Red walls make people feel tense and aggressive, blue can make us sad, while green spaces relax the brain. Studies have shown listening to nature sounds can even reduce pain. If you painted your entire room red, and feel more tense than you did last week – go get some calming neutral / green paint, and some taste.

Our primitive brains are built to exist in the wild, focusing on the physical world (with its many terrifying dangers). In our modern lives, with so much time spent tackling problems in our mind while sitting in closed, sterile environments, it's easy to get overwhelmed by the constant overthinking. Go hug a tree.

BE A TOURIST

Asides from annoying the locals and clearly looking lost and confused, being a tourist is a mindful way of escaping from your mind and feeling grounded. You don't have to go on a trip, you can try this exploring your local area! If you take your time appreciating every detail, focusing on your senses, not just rushing to get to your next destination, you can feel calmer.

For my local area that would involve noticing a defaced phone booth filled with questionable contact cards, and stopping to take photos of some huge rats eating the littered lunch of a clumsy commuter, but as long as I'm not in my head, worrying, it's a good thing.

No matter where you live, or the places you have to go, there will be things you can't control. If you learn to interact and relate to them from a different angle, and understand why they make you feel different ways, you can make them work for you.

EXERCISE: MINDFUL MOVING

Good for:
- **Finding focus**
- **Quieting stressful thoughts**
- **Feeling calm**

If you need a mental reset, by being mindful on your travels you can change how you feel in just a few minutes.

When you start moving, notice how you feel. Focus on your body and how it moves you forward and interacts with the air and the ground.

If your mind wanders, that's okay, just bring it back to focusing on your physical sensations.

Notice the details around you. The colours, the textures, the people – just be aware of these things without judging them or fixating on them.

Tune in to your other senses. The feel of the weather, nearby and faraway sounds, your sense of smell – don't worry about labelling them as pleasant or unpleasant, just notice them.

You will feel calm, more connected to the world around you, and less at the mercy of your mind. Remember this is something you can do anywhere at any time – it's your tool to use when you need it.

SLEEP

Sleep isn't just about our physical energy.
It's what powers and regulates our mind,
influencing our mood and our ability to cope
with life's challenges.

One bad night's sleep won't do much harm,
but a few nights in a row can take a toll, as
our brain struggles to maintain our energy,
motivation and emotional balance.

There are no magic solutions for instant sleep – there are some physical ones like anaesthetics or being punched in the head with a big red glove, but for all of us there are many things we can do to control our bodies and brains, to set us up for a good sleep tonight, and going forwards. It's not just about what you do in bed (oi) but the whole journey from the moment you wake up.

A broken body clock is tired several times a day

Although sleep might seem simple (something we understand pretty fast as babies, until we start screaming in the middle of the night), there's a lot influencing it that not enough people understand.

Our body clock, or 'circadian rhythm', dips and rises at different times in the day, determining how tired or alert we feel. People tend to be sleepiest in the middle of the afternoon (yes it's not just you, the post-lunch slump is a real thing) and when the sun goes down at night, or you've been awake for forty consecutive hours trying to finish one game of Monopoly. Our sleep system works best when we follow the rising and setting of the sun and, most importantly, are consistent with the time we try to sleep each day.

We evolved assuming we wouldn't one day be travelling around our entire earth so fast that the time of night and day can change. If you've ever experienced jet lag from travelling, that's what it's like to get out of tempo with your circadian rhythm. You know what new time-zone you have to adjust to, but your in-built body clock is convinced you need to follow the schedule you were on before.

Similarly, our bodies expect to get up with the sun and sleep once it sets. Whether you are a night-shift worker, a tired teenager, or living on that apocalyptic Arctic island where you only get one hour of light a day – we don't all live in this perfectly intended way, which makes our attempts to sleep more difficult.

As a teenager, I had a job in a warehouse where I started at 5 a.m. every Saturday and Sunday morning. It was the worst possible shift imaginable. It was the only place hiring, probably for a reason. Other than the mental health implications of one of these automated warehouse jobs, where your productivity and physical speed is tracked by an app and there's a complete lack of sunlight and human interaction, I did not plan my sleep schedule around it. I once went on a 'pub crawl' celebrating a friend's birthday and returned home at 3 a.m., deciding there was no point in sleeping. I walked to work, sobering in the winter air, and tried to just style it out straight through my shift. I ended up falling asleep while standing and almost destroying an industrial fridge stacked with yoghurt. On my break, I sat next to a table and closed my eyes momentarily and completely fell asleep. I nearly got fired. Don't be me – be realistic with planning your social life around your sleep schedule.

To any teens reading this, a moment of validation: teenagers naturally feel alert later at night, because their circadian rhythms change, making it hard to fall asleep until hours later, and hard to wake up early. It's not that you are procrastinating your responsibilities to socialise and sulk instead, you are definitely doing that, but you also have a biological excuse.

My mum, who I hope feels personally called out reading this, did not appreciate this biological excuse, as she physically pulled me out of bed every morning, exposing me to direct sunlight like some kind of hibernating bear mixed with a rapidly evaporating vampire. How do we expect teenagers to double in height and somehow learn to drive and memorise a thousand numbers for some test, unless they also get extra sleep? School hours should really be shifted for teenagers, to allow for a longer lie-in in the morning, taking learning into the evening – but that makes far too much sense, and humans enjoy putting people through the same suffering they endured in the past far too much.

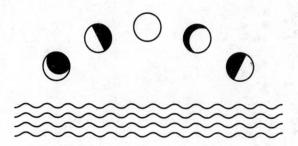

What's more important than the hours you sleep for is the quality of sleep.

How much of a good thing?

We all have different bodies, and require different amounts of sleep. Most adults need somewhere between seven and nine hours of sleep a night in order to function physically and mentally. Some people learn to live on four or five (unrelatable), and some claim to need ten, and are mocked by everyone in their life… but they actually might.

What's more important than the hours you sleep for, however, is the quality of sleep. The question is, how do you feel in the morning? An hour after you're up you should feel refreshed, energised, and not at all like if the bed was right there in front of you, inviting you to climb in, you could just wrap up in a cocoon and wake up with a body clock stranded and confused halfway around the world.

So, how can you sleep well tonight? And how can we make sure we're trained and qualified expert sleepers for the rest of our lives? The first step is routine. Like a dog expecting a walk, your body is sitting there impatiently wagging, waiting to learn when you'd like to feel tired every day. There's also 'sleep hygiene', which is not about showering before bed (although that helps) it's about everything you do to positively set yourself up for feeling sleepy and successfully slipping away when your head hits the hay.

This is really worth investing in, as a good sleep tonight makes you perform better tomorrow and even better equipped to enjoy life. Depending on how healthy your sleep schedule is, this may require extra dedication – but if you can get through the bed-bootcamp you will get through this night . . . by sleeping through it.

Operation unconscious

Get up – no matter how tired you feel, decide the time you have to wake up to tackle your day and don't stay in bed. As soon as you're up, get going and don't be tempted by the sheets.

Get moving – energy expenditure is one of the biggest influences on our likelihood of sleeping well. The best way to tire out an annoying hyperactive child is to play a physically demanding game, then give them a soft place to sit and watch them pass out. Big humans are just the same. The more we move in the day, the more we'll be craving the energy recovery of sleep. I reluctantly accept that the days I 'work out' tend to be the days I sleep easier, as opposed to the difficult days of twelve consecutive hours on a computer.

Get lit – (sorry, *light*). The more light our eyes digest in the day, the better our body clock will be at believing we have to sleep. The kind of light we experience is also important. Natural white and blue light keeps us feeling awake, so natural light is great for concentration in the day, but the default light from a lot of technology sends us similar signals. When the sun sets, the amber tones prepare our body for slumber, so any 'night mode' features on our screens that make the light warmer will help us to wind down. Bright light before bed is one of the worst influences, so to everyone like me who reads a screen with their head on the pillow for an hour before closing their eyes – yes, that is self-sabotage. As a child, as soon as I started reading a book, I would fall asleep with it in my hands. Books are beige. As long as the font size isn't straining your eyes, let these pages gently carry you to a land of dreams.

Switch off – try to avoid things that stimulate you before bed – apart from sex, actually, as afterwards that typically makes people instantly incapacitated.

Sex releases hormones (oxytocin and dopamine) that can help the body relax, reduces the production of stress hormones (cortisol), and is generally quite distracting. It can help your mind to disengage from the thoughts of the day, and engage with something else, and hopefully feel present (that effectiveness might depend on your partner's performance). You don't need a partner for the pre-sleep benefits of sex, however; for all the things we don't understand about mental health, and unhelpful behaviours we've evolved to do, there's one thing we're quite good at handling ourselves.

Other than that – anything that makes us excited, scared or alert will totally interrupt the pre-bed preparation our bodies want us to follow, so we should be aware of what we're doing and how it makes us feel. Some of us feel desperately connected to our work or social lives, and sleep surrounded by devices that threaten to violently 'ding' us out of a dream, which is why the silent treatment is essential. Just remember that you probably won't miss out on a life-changing moment by taking the minimum amount of time to close your eyes – you'll actually be the best you if you get some damn rest. Once you've prepared for bed, don't look at your responsibilities, the news, and the state of the world – or the latest conspiracy theory your strange uncle is concerned about – now is the time for rest. Put it on silent, perhaps put it in another room. You can investigate the new world order when you're feeling refreshed.

Try to train yourself with a sequence of activities you do before bed. It could be showering, reading, laying out clothes for the morning, stretching, spraying some strange lavender scented slime all over your pillow – which supposedly aids sleep but to me smells like a mysterious elderly woman – whatever gets you the opposite of going.

YOU SLEEP WHAT YOU EAT

For many of you, and me, we cannot function without coffee or tea. In the morning, the boost of some beans forcing energy into your body can help to get you up – but we need to be sure not to leave it too late. Any caffeinated consumption, energy boosters, or sugary snacks stay in the body for hours. We should try to avoid big amounts after the middle of our day as they will still be in our bloodstream when we try to sleep, confusing our bodies with chemicals of alertness.

I'm going to say from experience, any post-dinner desserts that involve coffee, matcha, or too much sugar, are outright evil temptations and traps designed purely to betray us in bed, for daring to enjoy life for just a moment. It's delicious, but you'll disagree it was worth it when you're sat upright in the middle of the night.

It's true that while some substances are stimulating, some are 'depressing' (and that means depressing your energy, not a depressing cake that went flat because you were impatient and opened the oven to look at it and let all the hot air out). Alcohol can certainly help you pass out, initially, but it's something your body struggles to process, and that disrupts your sleep for the rest of the night, so it's not a solution. The same unfortunately goes for rich, heavy or spicy food (basically everything fun in life) as the bigger and badder the meal, the more your body has to work to digest it. The 'pizza hangover' is real, because your body is in overdrive trying to break down that bread, and in the morning you realise you're saltier than the Dead Sea and much less hydrated.

This isn't to say that we need to live a life devoid of all meaning – if, like me, you essentially live to eat, just understand how it will make you feel, and fit it into the bigger picture of the great night's sleep you are preparing for yourself. Conscious choices of carbohydrate chaos.

NAPPING

Controversial topic warning: Some people swear by naps, some (I would never say who) consider it a freakish unnatural act that must completely throw you off – weirdos. Thankfully, the science can step in to mediate.

Napping is a good way to make up for lost sleep if you need it. A small afternoon siesta has been shown to boost energy levels for the rest of the day, but also take away your appetite for sleeping later, often making it much more difficult to knock out during the main event, or makes you wake up spontaneously in the night (like right after the nap). Consistent good amounts of quality sleep is healthier, and means you won't need to nap – but all of our bodies are different. If you can doze for small periods and you know it helps, you know your own body, just make sure you're still getting the consistent big sleep that you need!

Creating our caves

The place we retreat to for rest needs to be the best environment for getting a good sleep. We can't hibernate in a rave, and there's a reason squirrels start nut-hoarding in September – the perfect rest-nest requires care.

The first factor is light. Darkness sends signals to our brain that the sun is gone and it's time for sleep. Block out and turn off as much light as you can. The next important factor is temperature. I, personally, being descended from some kind of beluga whale apparently, am most comfortable in a frozen wilderness while cocooned in as much bedding as possible, so I look like a burrito. If it's anything higher than 16°C, I refuse to even lie down. If there's noise, we should get some ear plugs to block out the terrifying screams of the bin-foraging foxes having sex at sunrise. Comfort is very important, so we should do what we can to make our sleep space work for our bodies. Some of us are happy sleeping on the grass, some of us would detect a pea under a mountain of memory foam – but too many people pay no attention to their sleep comfort. If you're going to spend time or money improving *any* aspect of your life, sleep is one of the most important and fundamental. A good pillow makes all the difference. You will thank yourself for it when you wake up.

A SLEEP-ONLY ZONE

As discussed earlier, how we emotionally relate to our environment affects what we will be able to do there. If we associate the place we slumber with activities that don't involve closing our eyes and doing nothing, it will be harder for our bodies to get in that zone. As someone writing this sentence while laying somewhat like a French-girl being sketched (or beached seal) on my bed, I say this with full hypocrisy – but every time we use our bed as an office, a social space, or just a comfy place to watch or read things that make us feel excited or worried, we make it more difficult to doze. The only exception is the sexception; you know what you have to do.

MULTI-PURPOSE MATTRESS

If your bed is one of the only spaces you have, you can still make distinctions between the different things you do! You can help your brain differentiate day-bed from night-bed by trying things like wearing your day clothes, sitting in a different position or at a different end, propping yourself against a wall instead of pillows – or even just taking off the covers so it's more like a regular bit of day furniture.

Ultimately, if you're one of those people who sleeps successfully no matter what, then go off... to sleep. Use your bed as you please. If you find yourself struggling, however, being strict about these things helps to maximise our sleep efficiency and have the best chance when it matters.

THE FINE LINE

Feeling tired is not the same as being ready for sleep. Having a long day, physical exhaustion, or even mental stimulation can leave us feeling tired – but that does not mean our bodies are ready for rest, and if we confuse these signals and slip into bed, it can totally throw off our schedules. It's tempting to try to 'catch up' on missed sleep by going to bed earlier, but you might be surprised by how difficult it is if your body isn't expecting it yet, and end up just lying pointlessly for hours. If you succeed, you might throw off your circadian rhythm and get all the downsides of jet lag without any free mini-pretzels. Don't use this as an excuse to stay up all night if you feel like you can, though – decide the time and when it comes, give it a try. For the consistency of your internal clock, try to go to bed only when it's your time to sleep.

CLOCK-BLOCKING

Another counter-productive, counter-clockwise habit, is staring at the time. If we start doing mental maths about the time we have left before we know we have to wake, we will arouse our body with stress hormones and worry and make it harder to fall asleep. It's tough, but have faith your brain will know to switch itself off. You will be able to tell the difference between twenty minutes and an unsuccessful two hours, so don't sit there just watching the seconds tick by.

Go to bed with the aim of being there passively, not actively and alert. Let the sleep come.

Don't be a try-hard

Paradoxically, the harder you try to sleep, the harder it becomes. Many people stress themselves out by 'trying to sleep really hard' then wonder why they aren't drifting off as they lie, bursting blood vessels in their foreheads. Successful sleep is about lying in bed and letting sleep come when it's ready If you find you're still awake after twenty minutes, it may be a sign your body isn't ready, in which case you can do an activity (as long as it isn't too stimulating) (apart from that one) until you feel it's time. It may seem counterintuitive to get out of bed and read a book, but it also helps your brain's association of the bed as the place of sweet sleep. Trust your body. If you follow the signals you're being sent, and believe it when it's ready, it should work. Don't be concerned about your body betraying you with any midnight-activity delay; if your body clock decides the schedule and the sleepiness level, it shouldn't surprise you by demanding extra time tomorrow.

Sleep is about
lying in bed and
letting sleep come
when it's ready.

Wrestling the worries

For many people, a racing mind is the main thing holding you back from a good sleep. You could be feeling tired, on the brink of unconsciousness, then suddenly an intrusive thought of the single most worrying thing you can imagine gets sent to the forefront of your mind. This can actually activate the threat system in our body, so it's not just our minds racing, but our whole body goes into a heightened state, stopping us from sleeping.

This brings us back to the importance of 'being present' and not living up in your head, being remorseful of the past or scared of the future. During the day, when there are things to do and a world of possibilities in front of us, this layer of subconscious thought is kept at bay by distractions – but at night, when there's nothing between you and your pillow, these thoughts barge in and demand your focus. This moment of vulnerability is one of the main reasons 'night' is a difficult time for mental health. The night you need to get through, as it were. It can be overwhelming to suddenly be confronted with all of the things you didn't want to think about in the day, overlapping and competing for your attention – when in reality there's probably not much you can do about those problems if you're laying horizontally in a foetal position.

READ THE SIGNS

The quality of our sleep is often a window into our emotional health. If you try everything you can and you still can't sleep, it could be a sign of bigger problems with your physical or mental health, and it's worth talking to a professional to get their opinion.

This is my personal, biggest hurdle. I've been through periods of months, even years where as soon as I would almost sleep, my mind would stop me with worried, catastrophic thoughts, and only finally get some rest every other day out of sheer exhaustion. Thankfully, there are things you can do to stop these thoughts before they strike.

Talk it out – this is the number one, best solution for troubleshooting worry-ruined sleep. During the day, we don't want to think about our problems if we can avoid them, but it's much more likely we can either do something about them or at least talk to someone. We're usually not that great at solving problems by ourselves, with our single viewpoint, but sharing what's on your mind usually helps to break it down, see it from all angles, and often get a reality check on how scary it really is. Even if it's just for a moment in the evening, try talking to someone about what's on your mind, and it may pre-emptively put it to rest. If you have no one to talk to, you can write it down or say it out loud to get it out of your head and let it go. If talking it through leads you to having a plan for your problem, just remind yourself that you actually have a plan and hopefully your mind will be at ease. Even if the problem is complex and you don't quite manage to strategise a perfect solution, talking it through will usually help break it down and put it in perspective. Similar to saying the name of a scary spirit from a story, sometimes just acknowledging a worry removes its power. Don't let it haunt you by avoiding it until it goes bump in the night.

Use your tools – all the methods we've discussed for how to change how you feel can help you manage your mind to get you to sleep. Being mindful and stepping back from, and simply noticing and letting go of your thoughts. Slowing down and deepening your breathing. Relaxing your muscles, letting go of any tension from the day. Feeling physical in your surroundings, leaving your busy mind behind and focusing on how heavy you feel as you hopefully fall into slumber.

SLEEP SEMESTER RECAP

- Try to be consistent with when you wake up and go to bed.

- Have a routine of activities to help your body understand it's time.

- Control how much and what kinds of light you get in the day and at night.

- The more energy you use by moving, the more eager you will be to recover.

- Understand how the food and substances you consume affect your energy.

- Make your sleep-zone the best space it can be.

- Avoid activities that stimulate you in a non-sleepy way.

- Don't watch the clock or put pressure on yourself.

- Talk or write out your worries so they aren't on your mind.

- Use your mental health tools to relax yourself and get to sleep.

- Try not to snore.

FOOD

You aren't literally what you eat,
but you definitely feel it. What fuels
our body also fuels our brains,
and mental health.

The human brain only counts for around 2 per cent of your total body weight, but it uses around 20 per cent of your energy from calories. Thinking really is hard work. Fuelling your mind isn't just about getting enough energy from food – it's also *what* we eat for that energy.

For many of us, what we want to eat depends on our mood. I can tell you now that when I'm anxious, stressed or depressed, I'm not craving that garden salad. Our relationships with food and mental health are all different and unique to ourselves. Some people can't stomach the food they like when they feel low, some over-eat when over-emotional – yes, literally eating our feelings. The problem is that letting our emotions dictate our diet is usually totally counterproductive to making us feel better, and chaotic blood sugar levels are just as chaotic for our emotions.

If you notice that your eating patterns have changed for any reason, don't feel bad about it, it's natural for your body to want to react to your feelings. This part is not about how society defines the 'right' or 'wrong' way to be eating, for whatever right or wrong reasons – this is about simply understanding how nutrition affects your *mental health*, and how your emotional state can affect what you want to eat, so you feel informed, in control, and know what to do yourself to feel more balanced.

FOOD IS LOVE, FOOD IS LIFE

Our brains absolutely need fuel to help make decisions, concentrate and keep our mood level. Aside from that, however, eating is also a form of self-care. It can be good to remind yourself that doing something as basic as eating counts as looking after yourself – after all, some people, for many reasons, struggle to keep themselves fed, so we should feel thankful whenever we're able to keep ourselves healthy. People going hungry in our world is a mental health issue as well as a physical one.

We often see food as a reward, and therefore put a lot of emotional power into it, but food is not a bargaining chip, it is essential for us to stay alive. If we feel bad and our minds tell us we don't deserve to eat, or have food we enjoy, we are sabotaging ourselves emotionally and physically. Try to be aware of how you view food as a punishment or prize, and recognise instead that it's essential fuel that you always deserve.

A healthy attitude

Let's talk about the D-word. No, not 'depression' (we covered that), or 'Dan' – again this book isn't really about me, it's about you. Sorry, what? DIET.

There is a lot of pressure put on us, not just by the standards of beauty in our society and comparisons to our friends and peers, but by the idea of trying to 'eat healthily' and be healthy! Whilst of course we all understand the relationship between food and our physical health, too few of us appreciate the consequences of the pressure to be perfectly 'healthy' on our minds.

People who advertise certain foods and ways of eating to us are often not only dishonest about the full nature of their product's health-giving powers (how much exercise or surgery goes with that miracle superfood?) but they also have a subtle message that affects our mental health too. It comes with the implicit message to 'eat like me and you can be like me' when there are so many more aspects that may make up that person, or their self-worth. Just following someone's diet won't give you their whole lifestyle, or mindset.

A big portion of my emotional self-beating comes from food-related guilt. God forbid I have 'a chocolate' at any time in the day (it will probably be followed by an hour of deep shame and temptation to self-flagellate). It is possible to be reasonably conscious and perfectly content with what you eat and your physical health, and not put a ridiculous amount of pressure on yourself. You are not a 'bad' person if you eat 'badly'. Your value as a person is not based on what you eat.

A lot of unrelatable health plans and 'diets' recommended to us set us up for failure if we're anything less than perfectly committed to it, which leads to inevitable guilt. Trying to be 100 per cent healthy is just not realistic, and being dangerously driven by it can make us impulsively snap in the other direction if we fail – or at least deprive ourselves of joy. Some people just genuinely like healthy food. If your idea of a dream birthday plate is a pile of raw spinach topped with nutritional yeast – good for you! There's no shame in enjoying a naturally healthy diet, but if you don't relate, you also don't have to be like them. As long as we are fully aware of the contents of our food, how it affects our bodies and what our general diet is like, it is up to us to make whatever informed decisions make us *happy*. If we never did anything unhealthy, life would essentially be meaningless. Let us eat cake.

If we want, we can adjust the contents of our diet to make it more beneficial for our minds, to have more energy throughout the day, to feel more alert, or just to be sure we have the right amounts of vitamins and minerals to keep our health in check. This means eating plenty of brain-friendly foods like fruit, vegetables, beans, pulses, proteins and oils – and minimising the brain drains such as highly processed foods, caffeine, alcohol, sugar and salt. I'm sorry, that last bit was emotionally difficult for me to write.

PLAN AHEAD TO KEEP FED

If our lives are very busy or difficult, particularly if we're going through a period of bad mental health, maintaining a 'healthy' diet or even just eating can be hard. If you live with someone who can prepare your meals, that makes a huge difference. If it's up to you (and you are as hopeless as me) you may need any and all assistance available.

Recipes for success

Depending on your competency in the kitchen, you might be

aiming for anywhere between a mostly-not-burnt slice of toast, and a swan-sashimi with a truffle bisque mist – but we should try to have a bank in our brains of meals we know how to make without too much stress. Breaking out a cookbook can either be an amazing adventure for your fun evening, or the straw that breaks your back if you've had a long day, and the ten minute pasta you were promised takes two hours and sets your house on fire.

Meal prep is an essential life skill – don't be surprised by the moment you realise you need to eat. You can plan days or over a week ahead for specific meals, and buy just what you need. If you know you're busy or stressed, make stuff you can freeze or prepare in a flash. If you know you have bad habits, wait until you're full and fed and then don't buy the stuff you know makes you feel bad. If I shop when I'm hungry, it's complete annihilation. In the same way you should have 'easy access motivators' in your environment to help yourself day-to-day and avoid pitfalls, it should be the same with planning what you eat.

Keep it real

Just like the ideal of 'health', we can make ourselves feel bad about the quality of what we cook or eat. It doesn't have to be fancy – if it keeps you running it counts. Unless you're throwing a dinner party for your most judgemental friends, food is about getting something good into your body and there's no place for guilt or shame. The same goes for cost. I felt bad about eating that mostly noodle-based diet for years when I couldn't pay rent – it wasn't very healthy physically or mentally, but I lived through it. Nobody was judging me but myself, and I made some substantial savings. Just like we shouldn't compare our diets to people we may not personally be able to relate to, we shouldn't feel compelled to spend more than we need to, or judge ourselves for what we can make. You are feeding your brain, let yourself feel good about it.

Mindful meals

Depending on our circumstances and time, cooking for ourselves is a part of life that we can choose to view as a positive activity. For some of us who are not blessed in the kitchen, cooking can feel like a chaotic waking nightmare, but we can learn to make it an enjoyable part of our routine. If we pair it with other things we enjoy – listening to or watching something, socialising with the people you live with, even making a game or competition of it – we can look forward to this part of our days that we know is coming.

It's also a good opportunity to practice our self-care tools by being mindful with our thoughts, and indulging in our senses (in hopefully an enjoyable taste and smell experience) to bring ourselves out of our mind and focus on the physical world, so we don't cut our fingers off.

STOCKING UP

This might seem basic, but there is nothing wrong with planning for harder times. Whether you are planning for the next apocalypse with pounds of pasta, or just making sure you have snacks on hand for a stressful day, we should try to always have what we need for a time when we can't make or get anything else. Just don't hoard the toilet roll.

You are
feeding your brain,
let yourself feel
good about it.

SUBSTANCES IN YOUR SYSTEM

Want to know a juicy conspiracy? Caffeine is technically a psychoactive drug. It sounds dramatic, but that's just because #BigCoffee don't want us taking the tinfoil out of the drawer and putting it on our heads to think too hard. Many illegal substances in reality have a much milder effect on our bodies than normalised drugs like caffeine, alcohol, and even sugar – so it's important to understand what to sometimes not put in ourselves, or at least a bit less, if we want to feel better mentally.

Sugar – when we're stressed, our body releases a hormone called cortisol, which can cause an increase in our blood sugar (glucose). Stress can also block our body from releasing insulin, which can also contribute to high glucose levels in the blood. That's a lot of science coming from one scoop of ice cream.

Our impulse is to reach for sugary food when we're stressed – this is a quick fix to make us feel good instantly, but it will inevitably come crashing down, slumping our mood back to square one. We don't need to avoid sugar altogether, but we should go into it knowing how much we're having and how it is about to make us feel, then make us feel again a bit later. Foods that are high in protein like nuts will usually make you feel better, without the slump. They are just less fun. I respect that. If you're stressed and reach for the sugary snack, that's fine, if you know what's coming for you.

It happens the opposite way, too. If our blood sugar is too low we can be more likely to get angry or anxious, which is why it's important not to go too long without eating to keep up your energy levels. (There are some choices we can make about when and how we eat, like skipping breakfast, but it will have an effect on our mental health.)

The problem with sugar is it's hidden in almost everything from 'healthy juices' to literally bread. It's no wonder people, particularly children, can have such difficulty keeping a normal energy level throughout the day. Without being aware, we're spiking and crashing all over the place. Everything in moderation – unless you are knowingly and lovingly diving deep into that hyperventilation-bag of sweet and salted butter-caramel popcorn. Godspeed to you.

Caffeine – as well as giving us that bean boost of energy, caffeine stimulates our central nervous system, making us feel more alert, which as we know in our modern society usually doesn't reflect a real threat and therefore makes us stressed. It increases heart rate and blood pressure, which mimics many of the symptoms of anxiety and panic. For some of us with a high tolerance, a double espresso may be the only thing that gets us up and out, but if you are sensitive to caffeine, just a single cup could make you panic and shake. If you are sensitive to caffeine, watch out for it hidden in all kinds of food from tea, energy bars, chocolate, carbonated drinks, and even some common pain medications. When I think about all the coffee brand double-strength large size mugs topped with caramel sauce I've had, I feel very grateful that I am alive in this moment.

Alcohol – whilst alcohol has the power to relax our bodies and minds, it can very quickly make things worse. Being a 'depressant' it naturally brings in negative emotions. Initially it makes us disinhibited which can make us feel more confident or less anxious, but too much can lead us to feel anxious or depressed. Other than the physical hangover the day after drinking too much, we can feel very low in mood. It's important to understand what your personal relationship with alcohol is. This depends on your genetic disposition and physical health – as well as your mental health. For some of us, alcohol in moderation can be a consciously unhealthy way to have fun, but for others it can consistently lead to feeling bad physically, and be very dangerous mentally.

I feel fortunate to be a mainly clumsy and cringe-inducingly flirtatious drunk, who is most likely to knock over an urn or a priceless lamp – but I know from experience that if I start drinking in a negative mood, deliberately as a means to 'escape' or numb my mind, then it will only make me feel worse. Any substances that alter our mental state are dangerous if we're going through a time of turbulent mental health, and no matter how much fun they might usually be, we need to understand how to keep ourselves safe.

Note: each of these things are heavily addictive, and our bodies build up tolerances to and reliances on them. If you suddenly quit sugar, expect your energy levels to crash. If you detox caffeine you can get crippling headaches and want to sleep in the middle of the day. Quitting alcohol suddenly can be very dangerous – so whatever substance you may want to get under more control, do it in moderation and speak to a doctor or professional if you need to.

THIRSTY WORK

We might think our big brains are what make us so smart, but around 75 per cent of the tissue is just water, so we need to keep it hydrated. We lose water constantly through sweat, breath, and that convenient hole we have. Dehydration can be very dangerous, not just for our bodies, but our ability to make decisions to keep ourselves safe.

Just a small amount of dehydration can cause headaches, irritability, tiredness and loss of focus so it's harder to deal with challenges. On a day-to-day level, being well hydrated makes us feel more awake, alert and have a clear mind, which reduces the risk of developing depression and anxiety.

By the time you notice you're thirsty, your brain has already hit the point of dehydration, so we need to be proactive with our drinking. For adults we should drink a minimum of two litres a day, even more if it's hot or we're exercising – just don't drink it all at once. Try to have a drink available near you most of the day; you'll probably find yourself naturally drinking all the time. For reference, we're talking about regular water here. You can't down a two-litre bottle of something fizzing at midnight and expect to wake up with perfect mental clarity. Say no to bubbles sometimes, water is amazing. Learn to love it, live it, pour it all over your face and shake your head in pure ecstasy – this is the joy of being hydrated.

Eating your feelings

Much like we can learn from our activities and environment, we can learn from how the different things we eat make us feel. We're all different, so no matter what it says on the tin, try to think about how different meals make you feel, and remember that. Then, when you want to feel a certain way (whether that's alertness from biting a raw lemon, or totally comatose from an overindulged Chinese buffet), you know what you can do.

If you start trying to work out how different foods affect you, be patient with yourself and take your time. Don't instantly feel guilty for something that makes you feel bad, or for not being perfectly good – just make a note of what you discover so you learn more about yourself, and next time it can be a conscious effort.

MINDLESS EATING

That doesn't mean the moment you reach into a fridge at midnight, looking for something you-can't-quite-put-your-finger-on-but-when-you-see-it-you'll-know. We often eat 'mindlessly', which means we aren't focusing on our food, instead commuting, watching TV, or distracted by something in front of us. When we do this, we miss signals from our bodies and can eat because we're emotional or even when we aren't hungry – a good example is devouring an entire bucket of popcorn before a film even begins to play, or passively demolishing an entire bowl of crisps at a social event just because it was placed next to you. You mindless eating monster.

Whilst we don't have to eat 'mindfully', if we slow down and focus on the act of eating, and make it an intentional act (rather than something automatic), it's much better for our body and helps our brain to appreciate the moment and separate it from emotion. If you're concentrating on food you are more likely to know when you are really full, and even appreciate the taste better! Whenever I'm eating a meal I've been looking forward to (which for me is my only reason for making it through the week to Saturday night) I take an incredibly serious moment to remind myself to focus on the delicious food I'm about to eat – and I appreciate the heck out of it.

LEARNING TO FEAST

More than just a basic utility, food can be celebrated and shared with others in a way that connects our mind and body, and gives us positive reinforcement. In many societies around the world, food bonds people together and takes a central role in cultural celebrations – for a reason! Ask yourself, how can you make food a social celebration or even a solo spiritual moment?

Even as a reward to yourself, as long as your relationship and attitude towards what you eat is healthy, it's something that's part of our lives every day that we can look forward to. Ordering a pizza is a spiritual event for me.

EXERCISE: MINDFUL MUNCHING

Good for:
- **Appreciating your food**
- **Aiding digestion**
- **Emotionally relating to food**
- **Making the popcorn last longer**

1. Pay attention – try not to multitask. Just you, the food, maybe the person sat opposite you, but mainly the flavour sensation. Pay attention to every aspect of the food that you enjoy – the taste, the smell, the textures, the combinations of flavours and how it looks (unless it's a kebab). The chef will appreciate you.

2. Slow down – by eating slowly we help our brain to keep up with our body. Our brain takes around twenty minutes to realise when we're full, so we can eat more than we need or even really want. Also, when you slow down, you will probably savour the flavour better too. Remember to chew.

3. Listen to your body – your body's impulses will tell you to eat when you are hungry – your mind will compel you to eat just if you're bored, stressed or anxious. Try to separate how you feel emotionally from how your body feels physically. Really tune in to what your body needs, and usually your emotions will improve as a result.

4. Be consistent – our body learns our food schedule and any surprises can send signals of concern. If you skip a meal, your body will think something is wrong and send signals to your brain that will make you feel worse, even if you did it for a reason. Try to be as regular as you can and to keep your energy levels up throughout the day in order to keep your brain balanced.

5. Think about it – food doesn't magically appear. The way our food goes from creation to digestion is a result of people all over the world, from farmers to truckers, people picking and packing (teen-me at 5 a.m. collapsing into the dairy aisle), to the people who may have prepared your meal for you. Taking just a moment to think and appreciate the privilege of having food, and the fact it tastes nice, as well as providing a basic function, is something to be thankful for, and can be a moment of reflection that can calm you in your day.

MOVEMENT

Our bodies are meant to move. It makes
sense that our brains react to what we think
our bodies need – so to change how we feel,
sometimes we have to get up and go.

Imagine your brain, sitting up there, just waiting for some kind of signal to shoot some hormone into your body, or emotion into your consciousness, so you can rise to a challenge. Our brains are ready to handle everything from a marathon to hunting down a mammoth, to sprinting away from that sabre-toothed tiger (yes, it's still there) – but for some of us the biggest daily movement challenge is getting off the sofa to get a snack from the fridge. The good news is, if we want to help our mental health with our movement, we don't need to perform crazy feats of human endurance. Just a little, when you need it, can make a huge difference.

Let's talk about the e-word (at least it's not another d-word). No not 'electroencephalographically', that's the longest one. Exercise. The act of suffering, to apparently 'gain' something. For people like me who run, ironically, in fear from this, do not worry – for mental health it's much better to just think: 'movement'. One study showed that just an hour of walking, throughout the whole of your day at any point, can significantly reduce the risk of depression. You don't need to be an Olympic athlete, it's really just the difference between nothing at all and doing literally anything. Movement can be as effective as antidepressant medication in treating mild to moderate depression and dissipating anxiety. By releasing endorphins that numb our pain, we literally get high off our own supply. These feel-good chemicals can help relieve tension and stress, but even more than the supposed chemical 'solution' – just choosing to do any kind of physical activity is a distraction.

It's been shown that exercise can boost your productivity and creativity for over two hours afterwards, so it can be good to get you up for tackling that difficult mental challenge. Even on a small level, just going for a walk when in a depressive mood changes our environment, giving us something to focus on to distract our anxiety; it tires us out to relieve stress, and is one of the best ways to snap out of your current mental state to feel fresh! Who wouldn't want all these things? Me, apparently, every time I emotionally debate whether I really want to put on pants and go outside.

If you are someone who already gets a good amount of movement in your life, whether that's from daily travelling, walking a dog, or you are indeed one of those 'gym people' – the good news is you are already looking after your mind. If you enter a period of your life when, for whatever reason, you grind to a halt and don't get out of bed, you will probably notice a big difference to how you feel, and hopefully appreciate the importance of movement. For those of us who don't relate, however, there are ways to help.

If you haven't assumed so already: I do not like exercise. My relationship with it has historically only been motivated by shame and a pressure to conform. The more I learned about the positive benefits of movement for mental health, the more annoyed I became. I am a nerd, who was never encouraged to participate in sports as a child, and didn't really enjoy the idea of going outside recreationally. There are many people in my life who simply can't sit down for more than ten minutes, and have to go for that brisk run to start their morning – but I am worryingly content with spending an entire day slowly rotating between my bed, a chair and the fridge. This means my latent level of fitness is something close to a sentient ball of dough.

When I heard that I can move myself out of depression by walking down the street, I didn't want to accept it. The reality is that I definitely end up feeling mentally refreshed (and physically whatever the opposite of 'refreshed' is) then sleep better that night. People love to talk about the 'runner's high' of endorphins – as someone who has attempted to train for marathons twice, I wouldn't say I ever experienced this high, other than maybe a critical shortness of breath making me hyperventilate. I can't deny the positive impact, however . . . like the positive impact of being hit in the chest and limbs by a wrecking ball.

For people with any kind of physical injury or disability, life in general – and exercise – is understandably harder. When it comes to physical movement of any kind, or changing your scenery, hopefully there's something we are all able to do no matter how small. For anyone who considers themself able-bodied, it's something to be thankful for that this opportunity to positively influence our mental health is available to us.

IT'S NOT ABOUT LOOKS

It's important to separate the benefit of any kind of movement for your mental health, from using 'exercise' to change how you look. Just like with our diets, in our modern world we are bombarded with comparisons that can be toxic for our minds. We may have friends and family who have a completely different relationship with their minds / bodies and exercise to us, and see all these glamorous celebrities that live completely unattainable lives. When you see that person with a 'perfect body' on a big screen, they often dedicate their entire day to exercise, assisted by trainers and nutritionists, then have all the movie magic of lighting, lenses and editing to make them as pristine as possible. The fact is, we can improve our mental health with movement, in a way that works for us, without comparing ourselves to others.

If you want to transform your body physically, it can take a lot of time, dedication and pain to see the gains – but you can notice the emotional benefits of just a bit of movement straight away. Don't only approach physical activity from a desire to *look* good, remember to focus on how it can make you *feel* good. This is a much healthier mindset at the starting line and during the whole marathon of life. Who knows, if you become one of these people that does enjoy it, you may end up becoming an Olympian by total accident as a by-product of mental wellbeing.

Beat the blockers

'Blockers' are another word for the excuses we tell ourselves for why we can't do things. If, like me, you've never been very 'sporty', it's easy to tell yourself that you 'can't do' something, or that you will be bad at it. Try to talk back to this voice, and say that you don't have to be an athlete and it doesn't matter. If you find yourself reaching for reasons, try to find a solution. If you

Don't approach exercise from a desire to just *look* good, instead focus on how it can make you *feel* good.

don't have the right clothes or gear? Borrow some. You don't need the latest designer Lycra to do some light stretching on the floor. All you're doing is holding yourself back from feeling better!

THE BARE MINIMUM

There's a consensus that if we get thirty minutes of 'moderate exercise' five times a week, we're good. That doesn't have to be thirty minutes of climbing mountains or jumping across moving train cars, anything up from a 'brisk walk' counts. It's about doing something as opposed to being a permanent potato, rooted in place. You can even break it down to do ten minutes at a time; just make a start. The smaller you set your goals, the more you can enjoy your successes, and learn the positive benefits as you progress.

DON'T JUMP THE GUN

Make sure to be moderate and check in with a doctor if necessary, before making big changes to your physical routine. It's good to feel inspired, but if we try to go from zero to a hundred, we run the risk of injury, and setting ourselves up for failure which can hurt our motivation. Start small, build up, be patient with yourself, and make sure you're doing it for the right reasons.

Getting started

If you need every bit of motivation possible to move, a good place to start is what you enjoy. Do you like nature? Taking creepy pictures of people's dogs at a park? Hitting various balls with different parts of your body competitively? Hiking, climbing, team games – they're popular for a reason. They are enjoyable, supposedly. It doesn't even have to be stuff you would consider traditional exercise: dancing, gardening, aggressive housework and even a lot of video games these days can stimulate our bodies enough to change our mental state. Give yourself a reason to look forward to it! Don't doom yourself by imagining an obligation to row across the Atlantic; you can literally just sit in a chair flailing your limbs like a distressed starfish and that would count. The key is to be open to trying new things, instead of doing something once, hating it and swearing to never so much as wiggle a toe again. Be open to new experiences in case you discover something you love!

Time can be a difficult factor for many of us who struggle to imagine where we can fit physical activity into what might already be a crowded and stressful schedule. A good idea is to think about how to modify your routine to incorporate a bit of movement. Can you get off the bus one stop earlier? Commit to taking the stairs? Offer to walk the neighbour's turtle? Don't punish yourself by saying you will wake up super early, or rob yourself of an evening you are looking forward to. Just try to think about a little bit of action you can seamlessly squeeze into your day and hopefully you will realise that you feel better for it and want to keep it up.

If you don't have a space outside, or simply don't enjoy the birds and the bees, you can definitely do some kind of movement even if you're confined to a single bed – what I'm saying is there's no excuse, unfortunately. Just remember it's a good thing, you will feel better, you don't have to do much – and who knows, it might even be fun.

EASY MODE

We all look for excuses to put something off, so if we reroute our brains' habit circuits to make something seem as simple as possible, we're more likely to try.

Cues – you can set up cues that will trigger you to get into action. Like the 'easy access motivators' in your environment, anything to cut out time and remove excuses will help. Lay out your kit the evening before, get that music playing, have that drink at that particular time – when your brain sees certain things and appreciates a routine, it will start to accept it and put up less of a struggle.

Rewards – if we learn to link movement with a reward, we'll want to do it more. This can start with just how it makes you feel before and after. As we discussed in Part 1, if you note you feel stressed, and getting moving blows off steam – recognise and remember that. Even just rate your mood out of ten on each side of the activity, see how you feel mentally and physically, and remember it!

Treat yourself – give yourself a carrot on a stick. There's no reason to be saintly and altruistic – if you're making an effort to try something new, have something to look forward to afterwards. Whether that's a decadent bath, a snack, or permission to partake in some trashy entertainment. You've earned it.

Think about how you can make the moment of movement more enjoyable too, by listening to music, doing it with a friend, or going to a place you enjoy. We aren't trying to make our lives less fun by adding 'the burden' of exercise – aim to make getting up and moving one more thing you choose to do and look forward to because you like it. The key is, whatever you're doing, make sure you're aiming for something realistic and achievable. And once you've worked out what's right for you, try to apply 'cues' and 'rewards' to make it easy, and there you go – you'll be benching cars and winning international voguing contests before you know it.

REMEMBER THE MIND

Any kind of movement is a great opportunity to be mindful. Focus on your surroundings, be present (not up in your head), and tune in to your senses.

You can accomplish so many things at once, from changing how your body feels with some stimulation, to changing your mental state with a distraction – hopefully finding something fun to motivate you. It's one more part of life that influences your emotions and it's important to understand how, so we can choose to do things that will make our mental health better.

SOCIAL LIFE

Whether we consider ourselves social butterflies or socially anxious sloths, humans are built to be social creatures and we have an intrinsic need for connection to other people.

By far one of the most powerful factors for managing mental health is our connection to others. More so than any exercise, professional approach, and sometimes prescription – feeling that you are being listened to and appreciated can be the strongest support.

Strong social bonds give us a sense of belonging, protect against stress, boost our self-worth and confidence, and even improve our immune system! Our bodies and minds expect us to be surrounded by others, so if our mental health starts to make us less sociable it can be a downward spiral. In our modern world, which makes it increasingly easier to exist behind closed doors and screens, we need to be sure we're getting what we need from the people in our lives.

Closing the cave

When we go through tough times in our mental health, we naturally want to isolate ourselves. If we're low or tired, we might think it's too much effort to socialise. If we're struggling we might be ashamed to share how we feel and stop opening up to people who want to support us. This may feel like it's making life less demanding in the moment, but ultimately this avoidance can make us feel worse and, after too long, leave us feeling disconnected and unsupported.

Even if socialising seems like the last thing you want, there's a lot of value in forcing yourself through, because as well as a change of activity and environment, it can distract you and give you something all humans need. Being with others makes us feel part of something bigger. When we feel psychologically scared, sometimes just seeing other people can make us feel safe, and less alone with negative thoughts.

When I feel vulnerable I often feel like I don't want to be seen and judged by others, or expend the emotional energy to 'perform' like a normal human – but whenever I am forced into a social situation, it changes how I feel emotionally and is usually worth the effort. I'll just sit at the end of the dinner table sulking because I don't want to admit it.

But I'm built different

It's true that when it comes to the energy we use when we interact with others, some of us react in totally opposite ways. 'Introverts' tend to be drained emotionally by spending time with others and need to recover by spending time alone – often preferring to socialise in small, more intimate numbers. 'Extroverts' get their energy from spending time with people, and often look forward to the next opportunity to socialise. A common misconception is that these traits determine if someone is confident, or a good public speaker, but it is actually just about the effect socialising has on your energy levels. There are also 'ambiverts' which are supposedly a bit of both – but just like mental health, probably sexuality and definitely rainbows, social energy is more like a spectrum that can't be so easily simplified. After all, our attitudes to other humans and social scenarios depend on all the aspects of our psychological makeup that give each of us a different predisposition. You may think that extroverts have it easy, if socialising is naturally good for our mental health – but even the most introverted of us all (which is me by the way, I am the winner and certified most-introvert) still need quality human emotional connections. Introverts might need to recharge on a desert island for a month after briefly waving to a neighbour, but every now and then we need the reminder that we aren't alone in this universe and there are other voices than the one inside our head.

Just know that it's perfectly normal for your social appetite to be affected by how you feel. You might go through phases of needing to be surrounded by people, and then hibernating alone for the winter – it's all part of being a human being.

The social network

We get different things from the different relationships in our lives. It's not that we view other people simply as tools to give us what we want, but actually it kind of is exactly like that (you're not selfish if all living creatures do it). One person in your life can be good purely for distraction, having fun and letting go of worries. Others can be your emotional support system who you trust to listen and give you perspective. People often look for others who they can learn from, be helped by, or see as a stepladder to something we want to accomplish in life – pan out to look at the people around you, and try to recognise what it is about them that you value. It's also about not just accepting the way things are with your current relationships. We should aim to surround ourselves with people who make us feel good and help us grow; if someone holds you back in life or makes you feel worse, you can try to improve the relationship – or they might have to go. Granted, if that person is your grandma it may be more difficult to let them go, but as long as we understand how our social connections affect our mental health, we can decide how to manage them in order to help ourselves.

MAP IT OUT

It can be good to take some time to really consider the different people in your life, how much they mean to you, and how they make you feel.

If you picture your network as levels, or circles, start by putting yourself in the middle. You are literally the centre of your own existence, it's not big-headed to realise that. Those closest to you may be family, lifelong friends, or just people you trust with the big things – like the location of your snack stash, or passwords (brave). People in the middle we can like a lot, but perhaps not in the same emotionally intimate way. On the outer edges are people like neighbours and colleagues, who we may see frequently, but don't really do anything for us (sorry, Susan).

Relationships take time. Research shows it takes at least fifty hours of familiarity for an 'acquaintance' in your life to feel trusted enough to become a friend, ninety to be inner circle and a whopping two hundred to become a BFF. I feel tired just imagining

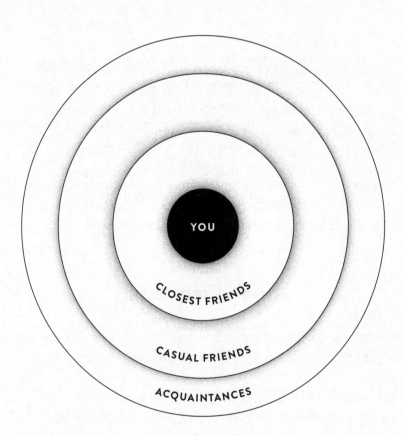

that; I'm going to ghost everyone for a week. This shows that meaningful relationships take time and energy, which can sound exhausting, but are a huge part of having a healthy mind.

Whether you are currently drawing chaotic circles on a napkin, or just visualising this, reflect on who you would put at these different levels of closeness to you. It's important to make sure you have people in that inner circle who you can rely on for support when you need it. Are you happy with the people who are closest to you, or are some of these relationships bad for you? Are there people on the outside who you recognise are great and want to be closer to? It's not about quantity, anyone who says they have sixty close friends probably doesn't have any. It's about quality – our mental health is not a popularity contest. Good news for me.

The quest is to make sure, however social we might think we are – or aren't – that our bases are covered, so as social animals we have that sense of belonging, acknowledgement and support.

Friend requests

If you want to improve your social life you can focus on either getting closer to the people already in your life, or finding someone new.

It's perfectly normal for relationships in your life to grow and change. A lot happens in life and our circumstances and personalities inevitably change with it. If you grow in different directions from someone who's always been a part of your life, that's okay. They might move town, change their jobs, get whisked away in a new relationship, and all these things can influence whatever bond you had with that person. If you find yourself evolving past the people in your life, it's normal for your relationship with them to change, and to find new people, or become closer to the ones you relate to now.

It's impossible for one person to tick every box in your life. If we have friends that aren't good for an emotional connection, rather than expecting them to step up and put pressure on them to be your mighty emotional rock, it's healthier to accept that that's not what they are good for. Comparing the relationship we might have with a person to relationships they have with others can make us feel bad if we feel inferior, or not as close to them. But we all have people we are intimate with, if we're compatible for certain reasons. It's about finding who can be there for you.

REACHING OUT

If there are people in your life you want to bring closer, or perhaps people who you feel you've drifted from – consider reaching out to reconnect! In busy times of life, it's natural to occasionally neglect some of the people around us, but it's not necessarily personal.

Identifying someone you'd like to be closer to is the easy part – human interaction is when it gets difficult. The reality is, we're all a lot more paranoid than we need to be. I constantly feel like I'm inconveniencing people, even if I'm not asking something of them. How dare I consider calling my closest friend just to say hi, what if they are doing something incredibly important and I . . . mildly inconvenience them?! The truth is, most of us aren't bothered by people saying hello, we're probably sitting around waiting for someone to. So go be that person. I say that as the one who throws his phone across the room if I hear any kind of noise representing a social event – but when I pick it up I feel happy to be wanted. If you're as hopelessly awkward as me, there are easy suggestions for icebreakers, from a simple 'hows u', to the 'reminder' strategy where you share a song or photo that reminds you of a good time you've had together. The other tactic is to be straightforward and say 'I've been thinking about you and hoping that we can reconnect and hopefully rekindle our connection so we can enjoy the mutual benefits of social connection' or, y'know, something similar but less like an alien who just took over a human body. People appreciate sincerity.

If your target is someone you want to lure closer to your inner circle, you can focus on what you think you have in common with this person, which will make your future-better-relationship so good! That could be doing a fun activity together, talking about something you're mutually passionate about, or having a deep heart-to-heart at 3 a.m. It can definitely sound a bit strange to look at social interactions in this slightly robotic-sounding and sinister way, but understanding what we (as complicated apes wearing shirts) look for and value in others, and how it affects our mental health, can perhaps help you understand your own feelings.

GET REAL

The most important thing when trying to find new friends – or get closer to current ones – is authenticity. If you change who you are to impress someone, it will never emotionally fulfil you. Know that! It may seem exciting or aspirational to chase after a friend, because they are popular, attractive, or can help your life and career, but every social interaction will be emotionally draining and stressful. When you lay down your head at night, you want

The reality is,
we're all a lot more
paranoid than we
need to be.

to feel you have friends that really know you. When a friend accepts you for who you are, you can relax around them and they will be a positive force for your mental health.

IT'S NEVER TOO LATE

If you've withdrawn from friends and lost touch with people, it doesn't mean you can't reach out and reconnect with them. You might be surprised at people's reaction if you just tell them you need them: turn it around and consider how you'd feel if someone you hadn't seen for a while reached out to you and tried to reconnect.

NOTHING TO LOSE

When we're feeling low and emotionally pessimistic, we tell ourselves things like 'they haven't contacted me for a reason' or 'they wouldn't like me anyway' but they are just excuses we make to avoid confronting our fears. So what if you spend time with someone and they don't like you as much as you like them? You're no worse off than you were before, you were just trying to improve your life and it's worth feeling proud of the effort. Don't give in to your fear-induced impulses – send that smoke-signal to your future soulmate.

EXERCISE: TALKING BACK TO YOURSELF

Good for:
- **Feeling confident**
- **Challenging obstructive thoughts**
- **Reframing negativity**

If you're doubting yourself and finding reasons to sabotage your social life, slow down and think it through. Is there any evidence it's true? Just because you want to feel it, doesn't mean it's real.

One of the best solutions is to reframe those thoughts:

I don't want to annoy them → I can just ask if they are interested

I just want to be quiet → I can be quiet with this person

I'm not feeling funny → I don't have to entertain this person

I'll bring them down → My friends want to be there for me

Talk back to your first impulse and see if you can be more reasonable with yourself.

A good way to review your relationships is to look at your circle and consider who lifts you up and who pulls you down.

Give and take

All relationships are a back and forth arrangement. You'll never both be equally as giving or needy as each other. Depending on what happens in our lives, we will go through periods of being there for someone, or needing their help.

Typically, when our mental health is good, we're able to put more into our relationships. You can give more attention, help, and bring people more joy. When we're low we have less energy to invest, and that's okay as long as we communicate with each other and know how equal and fair the relationship is.

A good way to review your relationships is to look at your circle and consider who lifts you up and who pulls you down. If you spend time with someone and often leave feeling happy, energetic or inspired – this is a good, compatible person for you to invest your time and emotional energy in! If you feel obligated (or forced) to spend a lot of time with someone and leave feeling drained, sad or put down – it may not even be noticeable conflict, but you should recognise it and protect yourself.

Some of the people in our lives are not so easy to separate ourselves from. If we're committed to living, working, or sometimes even socialising with people who are bad for us, we can't simply escape. Learning to minimise and manage the negative effect people can have on you, by not indulging their destructive behaviours, or quietly distancing yourself from them, is difficult but necessary if they wear away at your mental health.

The worst thing is to suffer in silence, so while one person may be hurting you, make sure there is someone you can share your feelings with. Each person we feel close to is a tether that grounds us to reality and makes us feel we are not totally alone.

GETTING OUT THERE

If we need more people in our life – not just soulmates who stand the test of aeons, but maybe just some mates to mingle with – it can feel daunting. Where do you start? The reality is most human relationships come from the places you're forced to be. Your family, your neighbourhood, school and work. The idea that we all have perfect soulmates out there waiting for us that we will never find in an ocean of billions is not realistic. Not because you will never find them, but because magical perfection probably isn't real, and one of the many people you will inevitably bump into in life will be that just-fine amount of compatible to tick your box.

Plenty of people are lifelong friends with the people they met as children – you don't all have to be perfectly alike, and sometimes time and tumultuous experiences are the best bonds for long-term relationships. If, like me, you tend to constantly roll to new pastures and struggle to keep in contact with the past, it can leave you dangling when you're older and are inevitably less likely to be forced to spend all day with random people. If people we see at work or class every day can also be our friends, that can be great. However, it's just as likely that these people we see all the time can remind us of things that stress us out, or prevent us from getting close if it is

DON'T BE SILENT

If we're in a situation that is emotionally or physically abusive, it can be hard to disentangle our past positive feelings for that person with the current reality of their behaviour. The truth is, none of us should have to tolerate a situation that puts us at risk of harm or makes us miserable.

Abuse within relationships can be subtle. It might include behaviour like them controlling who you see or what you do, criticising you for minor things, repeatedly devaluing your opinions, or 'gaslighting' – where they manipulate you to question your own thoughts, memories and behaviours (maybe even your own sanity). It can feel difficult to confide in someone else. Abusive people often make threats about what they'd do if you were to leave them, or how talking to someone outside of the relationship would be a betrayal. However, confiding in someone else, whether that's a friend, colleague, family member or a professional, can be an important first step in finding safety.

We all want to be able to 'save' people or relationships, but if the burden is being put on you it isn't fair. If you enable or excuse their behaviour for any reason, it can sometimes stop the other person from confronting what they need to deal with. It is not a betrayal to stand up for yourself or remove yourself from the situation, and with some toxic behaviour that can be the intervention the person needs.

The priority is to be safe. Don't be silent. Reach out for help if you need it.

not a relaxing environment. This is when we have to look outside of our default-life to find fresh fish. It's a big sea out there.

A good place to start is your passions. Whatever you enjoy doing, search for a community that is looking for more people to share the love. If you like sports, join a team. If you like music, advertise for that garage band that will take over the world in ten years. If you enjoy roleplaying as a dragon, I'm sure there's some people in a basement somewhere who are desperate to join you. It helps when you have similar interests and shared topics of conversations for an instant connection. Even if you don't end up personally clicking with someone, you're still doing something you enjoy! Anything that involves teams or building a community together is great, as working on a common goal gives you a bigger sense of belonging. So what if you've never kicked a football before? Someone in the club has to design the T-shirts and pass out warm drinks when you're standing on a freezing field first thing in the morning. Volunteering is another great way to feel part of something, proud of yourself and meet people with a similar mindset.

To me, it can be the most terrifying idea in the world – but sometimes we just need to put ourselves out there. When I started making a conscious effort to fix my friend zone, I reached out to other performers I admired and even total strangers in some video games I played. It wasn't all a success. I was left on 'read' a lot, to which others tried to tell me they were probably just busy – I knew the truth. Not naming names, but a few figures clearly wanted to dive into something other than light conversation and were suddenly less interested when 'mutual interests' were the only thing I spread on the table. Sometimes I got to know people that I quickly realised after two drinks, a late night goblin-slaying session, terrified or disturbed me on a fundamental level, and I had to come up with a fantastical excuse to distance myself from them forever. It was mostly worth the struggles as from the social shotgun I fired at the wall, despite a few misses, I found a fellowship of fair-weather friends to keep me entertained and a couple of companions I can now confide in and count on – and who knows when I might really need that, or need to be there for them.

Open for business

If we're actively looking for conversation and communication, we should be aware of whether our body language can make us appear closed off or open to connecting. If you cover your eyes with sunglasses, ears with headphones, and crane your entire face down into some papers – you're telling people not to talk to you. Granted, if you're having a vulnerable mental health day, feeling introverted, or just caused total chaos down your shirt by spilling lunch, this may be an intentional and highly lucrative avoidance strategy. As long as you understand how we're coming across.

One of the most profound pieces of advice I received was to leave my door open the first time I lived in a communal space. Feeling shy, I wasn't sure if I really wanted visitors, or to advertise my space as the 24/7 social hub – but I was reassured that anyone new to an environment is in the same boat. This applies to starting a new class, job, or moving to a new town. If you're nervous, so are they. Being the first one to break the ice usually causes a collective sigh of relief, and helping others can help to relax you. I also had a huge bag of marshmallows to share with people that passed by – essentially bribery – but it was a good icebreaker and a first impression that definitely set their expectations way too high for me.

TRUST FALL

If we want to turn a stranger into a life partner, it's not just about time spent together – it's about trust. For trust to form in a relationship, there needs to be mutual vulnerability. This doesn't mean instantly admitting to that murder you got away with, or taking compromising photos of them accidentally littering as kompromat – just showing a small bit of openness and honesty signals to someone that they can relax and worry less around you too. Rather than pretending to be brilliant and brave and practically perfect, occasionally sharing your concerns and flaws can make you more likeable and relatable to others too. When you have shared rises and falls, been there through change, and just done the time with someone, you will develop the trust necessary for them to graduate to the inner circle.

If you've been burned in the past, either by bullying, betrayal or rejection, it makes sense your mind's instinct is primarily to protect itself and avoid opening up. Just remember that every person is different, and if you are in a new environment, doing a new activity, or are in a new time in your life, the circumstances should be different and you can try again. Give new people a chance to not repeat the actions of those from your past. For every kind gesture and act we're capable of giving to someone else, there is a person who can return that to you.

Give new people a chance to not repeat the actions of those from your past.

SOCIAL ANXIETY

It's common for all of us to experience 'acute' anxiety in social situations, if we're new or nervous – but there is an elevated state of social anxiety which is technically classed as a disorder (*social anxiety disorder* or *social phobia*). This too can be common, often appearing when you're an awkward gangly adolescent, but too many of us don't recognise that this anxiety is a common problem and just assume we are defective. There is a difference between being generally awkward, and having social anxiety.

I'm the first person to admit every awkward thing that's ever happened, such as recently when I said 'after you' to an elderly neighbour in an elevator and proceeded to press the 'close' button instead of holding the door open and suddenly almost crushing them, much to the horror of several other neighbours who now hurriedly close their doors as I walk past. I share this as not only does it help me vent, but apparently people like to laugh at my pain. It's okay to enjoy relating to others' socially inept moments, but we should never glamorise or celebrate real anxiety. It's not a personality trait; if it is seriously holding you back in life, you have a problem. But there are things you can do about it.

The main feature of proper social anxiety is the fear of embarrassment and judgement. It's not just being nervous of public speaking, but an all-encompassing feeling that can lead people to struggle in basic social situations or avoid them totally out of fear. The good news is that it can be easily managed.

Taming social anxiety

- Social anxiety thrives on avoidance, so try not to avoid the social situations that bring you fear. When you join these situations, try not to hide behind any walls of humour or quietness, just be you.

- Test out your predictions. If you predict you'll screw up a presentation, go redder than a flaming tomato, and everyone will laugh, that's a testable hypothesis which you may learn from or prove wrong.

- In socially anxious situations, our attention turns inwardly on ourselves, concentrating more on how sweaty we may look than the reality of the situation and what others are thinking. Try to be present, focusing on your surroundings, and the anxiety may fade away.

- Remember that in the real world, the older you get the less likely people will be to laugh at social incidents, unless they're assholes. Don't default to fears from your past, let people surprise you with their kindness – and if not fuck 'em.

If your fear of being judged in a social environment is holding you back from basically functioning daily, or stopping you from doing things you enjoy, it may be that your anxiety has tipped into social phobia – consider seeing a professional to discuss therapies that can help you overcome this anxiety so you can start to enjoy social situations rather than fear them.

Social media

Technology has completely changed how the human race socialises with each other. We've gone from telling folk stories around the fire, to the printing press, television, and now we have our grandparents tagging us in cringe chain-letters when we're trying to look cool on our perfectly curated public profiles.

The internet has allowed us to reach outside of our physical environment in ways that can be a lifeline – by finding information about the world and yourself, which you may not otherwise discover, by finding communities of like-minded and supportive people, and even making meaningful connections. The issue is that there are some things that we can't get without real-life connections, and ultimately it is physical support that is the most powerful and comforting.

It's safe to say, as someone who lives almost entirely online, that most of my relationships are international internet ones. The people I text chat, call, look at pictures and videos of, and even spend most of my recreational time socialising with digitally, are an incredibly important part of my life, and make me happy – I know, though, that the handful of people around me in person are the ones I can count on in a crisis.

When we feel like all our emotional needs are being met online, it makes us less likely to make the (much bigger, harder, slower, less cool) effort to meet new people in person, but we need these people too.

SYSTEMS OVERLOAD

The fact is, we were not built to process so much information and interaction. Our sensitive brains, patiently waiting for a single physical challenge right in front of us to respond to, can't comprehend the bombardment of emotional messaging that waits to explode out of our screens and send our systems all over the place.

When we see a friend in person, or enjoy a bit of attention in our days, we get a dopamine hit that rewards us for being social, as that will probably keep us safe and sane. On social media, every single notification gives your brain the same signals, and this non-stop geyser of good vibes is addictive. Why risk only having one interaction by walking to the park, when you can scroll on the toilet, getting constant attention for hours?

The other part of our brain being assaulted is the threat system. When we see a 24-hour news cycle of amazing and awful events, it's exhausting for us to emotionally relate to. When we can no longer escape from our daily environments, the emails from work, or the people from class leaving comments, it means our brains can never turn off from the times and places where they are stressed. Our brains need time to recover from this emotional exhaustion.

The other dystopian side of this tale looms towards influence, social status and all-powerful algorithms, which combine to create a centrifuge of chaos that we're all subjected to, but that may not be something you can tackle right now, so no worries?

SAFELY BEHIND A SCREEN

We all have negative impulses. When we feel bad, our base instinct can be to hurt others to bring them down to our level. If we're jealous, sad or angry, we want to sabotage people who have the audacity to not wallow in our same sorrow. The truth is that this does not make us happy. Indulging in this toxic behaviour leaves us ultimately feeling sad and shameful. It can be hard when we feel we don't have support in life, or are struggling in silence, but we need to make the effort to deal with our problems personally and not take out the pain on others.

In the real world, people are generally better at this because of, well, consequences. People don't generally say to their colleague's face what they may send online to a public figure in ALL CAPS (!!11!! >:O etc) at 3 a.m. The more anonymity a person has, the more they feel they can get away with negative behaviour. Psychological studies have shown that all of us, given the power of anonymity and immunity, are more likely to indulge in harmful behaviours in an attempt to make ourselves momentarily feel better. The internet, to different degrees, gives all of us this power and responsibility – but we have to be better than our worst instincts. The less real someone's online identity is, the less you can trust that what they are saying is true or emotionally reasonable. People will be cynical just because they've had a bad day, they will be angry and impatient because they experience injustice in their lives. Sometimes when we see how people treat each other online, it can make us feel extreme emotional reactions, as we have expectations for how people act when they actually care about social consequences in-person. This means we all have to remind ourselves to take everything we see on the internet with a grain of salt. Stand back and think – this person's perspective is more likely to be emotional than honest.

I developed a thick skin from being born in the fires of the internet from a (probably too) young age exploring dial-up internet unsupervised, then later being catapulted into a career where comments from strangers rained on me like a microburst of blunt opinions and unfiltered emotions. Reading the casual use of slurs, unmoderated aggression towards anonymous strangers and a general lack of accountability definitely made a mark on me. As my daily job started to involve regularly diving into comment sections, it was not unusual to find a random troll wishing death by a rain of scorpions upon my family, or someone obviously just trying to wind me up by saying that one thing I clearly wanted to avoid. 'Windup_Merchant_2004xD' didn't actually think my awkward emo haircut made me look like a hedge, but they knew saying it every day would annoy me – and they succeeded. Rather than reading the lesson about letting go of what I can't control in some book, which would have been helpful, I developed that ability naturally as a result of being worn down for years. Hey, it's still growth! It took me a while to realise that the silent majority of humans are not the ones posting comments. People with reasonable opinions, a respect for feelings, and desire to be genuinely productive, aren't the ones being proportionally represented. It's far more likely to see the people looking for an opportunity to act in bad faith behind the safety of a screen to make someone else feel worse.

This means that most humans aren't monsters, as you might sometimes believe, we're just more likely to see the people who are hurting, on their worst behaviour. It can be hard to have sympathy for the struggles of someone who chooses to strike out if you know you wouldn't do the same, but it may help to at least rationalise their behaviour by appreciating what they may be going through in their lives.

It's important to develop your sense of when people aren't acting earnestly, and avoid giving it too much of your time or emotional energy. This doesn't mean, however, that we should put ourselves in a bubble that only reinforces our opinions, or we will lose our objectivity and won't be able to deal with confrontations and challenges when they come.

Sometimes, people can behave badly online and deserve consequences online. It's a healthy mix – just like the real world. Be aware of what's going on and being said, but have the resolve to filter out what matters and know when to step away. There are good people out there, I promise, you just might have to belly-crawl through the mud to find them.

FEAR OF MISSING OUT ONLINE

It's no secret that many of the social sites we use every day are deliberately designed to keep us addicted by showing us the most sensational things, which they know play to our human instincts. Rather than giving us a realistic reflection of the people and the world around us, we're only shown the highest highs and the lowest lows. We feel pressure from this non-stop barrage to portray our lives as perfect. After all, if it's hard to open up about vulnerabilities in person to a close friend, it can be terrifying to be the first one to make yourself appear fragile on the internet.

This creates a destructive cycle where we only update people on our best news. I got a promotion! I got married! I'm having my dream vacation! People are less likely to say that they are struggling with work, that they had a fight with their friend, or post a picture sitting in their desk cubicle as they drink out of a stained coffee cup. This completely distorts our perspective of reality, so we start to feel like we're the only ones with problems – we need to remind ourselves that often what we see online is just the questionably airbrushed surface of someone's life. Behind the screen we're all people and we've all got problems.

When I hit upload on my 45-minute epic 'Basically I'm Gay', I was braced for impact. Not only did I expect misunderstanding, misrepresentation, cynicism and doubt about my sexuality and my story, (and people's problematic opinions on queer rights) – I just assumed that on the internet, being honest about feeling bad would result in rejection. Thankfully, this wasn't the case. In regards to sexuality, certainly a lot has changed in the world for the better since I was a child – and the internet is even a much nicer place than the dial-up days, but it was as if my open vulnerability cut through the mirage of people's internet personas and we were really connected. When I explained my story, how I secretly felt all these years, and why it took until now for me to go on this journey, people were supportive and empathetic. Sure, there were probably a few assholes if I looked hard enough to find them, but why would I? It's always nice when humanity positively surprises you.

The digital detox

If we feel like we associate social media with negative emotions, such as envy, inferiority, stress about news and politics, or exhaustion from social drama, we need to either readjust our relationship with technology, or probably go on a break. Just like in times of bad mental health, when we can spend too much time 'in our heads', worrying to ourselves in a constant loop of scary negative thoughts, too much time spent online can make us focus more on this digital world of imagined voices than the real world around us. This dissociation is not natural, which is why reminding ourselves to be present in the physical world, and manage our time online, is a crucial skill.

You don't have to throw your technology into a flaming barrel and live alone in the outback to escape the negative side of social media, just tone it down a bit. As one of the world's leading experts in not having a life, and learning to live not just integrated with technology, but featured right in the centre of the digital panopticon for a decade, I have learned (the hard way) how to help myself.

Curative content

I know it sounds wild, but unlike our physical world, the benefit of the digital one is we have the power to control what we see. If something makes you feel bad, see less of it. If it makes you feel good, subscribe for more of that newsletter and make it a constant force for good in your life. It should be easy, but we're all a bunch of sadistic perverts who can't help looking in Pandora's Box.

We have the fear of missing out on whatever is popular, but if bad news and even worse politicians start taking up too much of your brain – reach for the mute. It's not blissful ignorance to curate your feed to make yourself feel good. The news is there if you really want to peek into the pit of chaos, but you don't need to shove it into your face all day. Likewise, if there are friends, colleagues or celebrities you feel obligated to follow, but they make you feel frustrated or upset, you really don't have to see that either. If it's someone you can't so easily cancel your subscription to (like the time I 'unfriended' my grandma and caused a family rift for about a month) you can always 'mute'. Muting is fantastic. Unlike blocking, which can give a troll attention or make the conflict obvious, if you mute someone – whether it's a spectacular idiot or just a friend getting on your tits– they will never know you elected to spare yourself from whatever they have to say.

Give yourself permission to miss out on the things that are bad for your mental health. Just because everyone is obsessed with some scandalous drama, doesn't mean you have to damage your brain cells too, or feel yourself succumb to the toxicity by dwelling in that dark, dramatic place. There's a lot of stuff out there on the web and a lot of it is good for you. That doesn't just mean stuff that's dramatic and sensational – really think about what makes you smile. What are you passionate about? What inspires you? What leaves you feeling more energetic and hopeful? Seek out content that celebrates the things that excite you in life, and keep you curious and growing. Just don't end up in that bubble of unrealistic perfection that encourages your worst behaviours.

As with all the other aspects of life you can change now to set yourself up for better mental health, taking the time to analyse your relationship with social media. What makes you feel good or bad? Does the dopamine hit of attention last, or does it fizzle away, leaving you feeling worse than you did before you looked?

You're giving yourself square eyes

If someone tells me to spend less time online, I roll my eyes, think 'ok boomer' and go back to comparing myself to perfect supermodels and feeling shameful. The truth is, we're all a bit addicted to our devices and sometimes intervening to make us put down the screens and see the world around us isn't just a way to stop that elderly person nagging you – it can also be a huge help with regard to our mental health, and developing the tools we have to make ourselves feel better. You can't be mindful when you're reading about breaking news or the latest pop culture discourse; you won't be physically present if you feel totally absorbed by a trending timeline with thousands of people screaming at each other. It's information overload for our poor brains, and sometimes they need a break.

Even if it's setting time limits on your devices, or being diligent with what time of day you dive in, try to plan times to give the narration in your head a rest, and experience being a real, physical being. We will probably have our consciousness downloaded into avatars in the near-cyberpunk-future so we should appreciate things like headaches and insects while we still can.

To understand how technology affects you, take some time away and note how different you feel. I've taken time away from looking and posting online, and it made me calmer, less anxious, and more productive. I can't really go without it, as my career and life would just collapse into a meaningless abyss, so I accept that I've somewhat tied myself to this never-ending nightmare, and learned instead to curate my content, manage my expectations of humanity, and know when to put the screen down and just be real.

SHARING IS CARING

Whether online or in real life, there are plenty of people who are willing to listen, and who want to help – asking for help can be the hardest part, the part where the stigma around mental health can hold us back. Remember that we all have emotions, all have difficult thoughts and times in our lives where things are going down and we need help. If you need help, ask for it. Whatever you are going through, people will relate and we shouldn't feel embarrassment or shame for speaking about something universal.

You own your
story, it's your
choice how much
to share.

If you're not used to asking for help, it can be intimidating to open up and put yourself in a vulnerable position. I'm one of those people with trust issues, so I very rarely speak my mind. Finding people I know I can trust is important as – other than the completely random strangers who I apparently share intimate details of my 'story' with (hello, how are you?) in my day-to-day life – I play my cards close to my chest. The problem with being incapacitated by the fear of inconveniencing others, or betrayal, is we never assert our needs. If we spend too much time being 'people pleasers' or doing things 'for others' (as much as giving truly makes us happy), if you never do things for yourself, it will slowly drain your energy, resentment will rise, and ultimately you will feel worse. This is why it's important to talk to people on your terms, in a way that feels right for you.

Think about who you might want to talk to, who you can trust. Consider how much you want to share – you don't have to give someone all the details to let them know you're not okay. You own your story, it's your choice how much to share.

For me, this is a dance I've dabbled with many times. From firstly opening up to a college counsellor about my mental health affecting my ambition to study, to asking doctors and therapists for help with these intimate issues, to publicly sharing the story of my struggle with depression and, my biggest moment, coming out as a not-raving queer. It may be relatable, if not too helpful, to know that I don't find it easy. This applies to any scenario in life where you have to have 'difficult conversations', from opening up about mental health, sexuality, gender identity – to ending a relationship or quitting your job. Learning to do what's right for you, even if you have to manage someone else's reaction, is an essential survival skill. Find someone, talk to them, and you will feel a weight lifted.

Choosing the moment

To make it easier to muster up the courage, you can think about the best time and place. If you try to open up about anxiety as a friend is closing their front door, they might not have time to process and appreciate it. Find a meaningful amount of time, a safe and stable location (not about to go over the edge on a rollercoaster) where you feel relaxed.

CONVERSATION STARTERS

Whether you're texting, calling, or conversing in real life, there are ways you can comfortably segue into what may be an uncomfortable topic:

'Do you have a moment today? I'd like someone to talk to.'
'I've really not been feeling my usual self lately.'
'I've been having a tough time lately.'
'This is difficult for me to say but I've been having a hard time. I think it would really help if I could talk to you.'

Don't be too ambiguous, be clear with what you're feeling and what you need, and remember that these moments usually bring you closer and make you feel better. So go for it.

Start small

You don't have to jump straight in and blurt out something blunt and intense, you can break the ice with something else, like a text. No matter how it feels socially, if it is manageable to you emotionally it's probably worth it. Anything that isn't in person understandably comes with a delay, so don't leave a voicemail if you need urgent help, but it can make the awkwardness factor less of an obstacle.

Starting is usually the toughest part, so don't think too hard about how you get into it. Even the clumsiest start will roll you in the right direction.

On a final note, try not to expect too much from other people – remember they're human, and they won't be able to read your mind or come up with magic solutions, so you might need to spell out what's wrong, and even tell them what you need from them. And not everyone knows how to respond when they see others are upset, so try not to interpret any silence, or awkward answer, as not caring – they might just not know what to say.

As we know, I rather infamously came out to my family via email. I figured I supposedly owed my family the respect of a private conversation before I told the entire world at once. I initially intended to tell my family over the holidays, so the day after Christmas when the whole family were sitting casually nibbling on some cheese, my moment came and I just couldn't do it. Understandably, like admitting to anything you've been struggling with, I was afraid of expressing vulnerability, unsure of their reactions, and mainly felt like I didn't want to ruin everyone's festive day by making it all about me. I tried again on a birthday, at Easter, then eventually it just got a bit silly, so I sent the email entitled 'Basically I'm Gay' and that was it. It was completely ridiculous, but it worked! The ice was broken, more like a glacier imploding really, and the instant phone calls after I hit send reassured me that I'd successfully cleared the first hurdle. Don't avoid asking for help, or sharing what's on your mind, because you don't know how to start. Throw a note folded into a paper plane and run out of the room if you have to. As long as you start.

RETURN THE FAVOUR

The more you learn about mental health, the more I hope you feel you can be there for the people in your life. One of the best ways to make ourselves feel better is to help the people we love, or to contribute to society in a positive way. Look out for signs that people you know may be struggling and give them the help that you may wish you could get yourself – just remember that you can't help others before helping yourself first. Like an oxygen mask on a plane, you won't be good for much if you're running out of air as you prioritise everyone's needs over your own. If you really want to help others the most, you need to be the best, most functional and productive version of you, in order to be the best help for others. We all know people like this, who do everything for others and never take a moment for themselves – force them into a damn spa. If that's you being described, genuinely well done for being nice. Now go away and prioritise yourself for a change.

By now you should feel you have the basic tools to address how you feel if you need an immediate change, and understand the areas of your life that you can control. When you understand the relationship between the things you do every day, and how you feel, you can make small changes that will eventually build up to be a strong foundation in your life.

If you try to make any changes, give yourself time, patience, and allow yourself to experiment and learn about how changing these things makes you feel. Focus on what stands out to you most so that you can learn and be better at managing your mind.

Part 3

THE DAYS
AFTER THAT

Part 3

THE DAYS AFTER THAT

Once you feel you have the tools to take care of yourself in a tough moment, and you've done what you can to improve the world around you to give yourself the best chance, you have created the time and space to think about the bigger things that will keep your mind healthy in the long term.

Our minds are the culmination of a lifetime of experiences, emotions, thought patterns and habits, that dictate how we are likely to respond to the events that pop up in life. If we can step back and ask ourselves why our minds work as they do, how we learned these habits, and what is a helpful way to treat ourselves, we'll be better equipped to rise to challenges and have a more productive mindset.

Through my journeys of self-understanding, I've come to recognise myself as an incredibly talented saboteur, who can reliably have the most unhelpful reaction to any given situation. Most of my emotional responses to situations stem from attitudes I developed from a young age, to generally feel ashamed, tolerate abuse, and fail to assert my needs. While my mindset is quite successful, there's a lot of baggage trying to pull me down – it's something I have to keep in check constantly. This journey started the moment I first thought about why I'm like this. Simply by starting to think about your own relationship with your mind, you will immediately have that small bit of perspective that can make a difference.

We're all tempted to mentally coast through life, mainly worrying about the pressures of the day-to-day, and not to take the effort to dig a little deeper. It's not appetising after a hard day to spend your free time staring deeply into the mirror of your mind, trying to analyse yourself like a confused Labrador who just walked nose-first into a screen door. It's easy to remember the past and have a good moan about all your regrets, a lot more difficult to try to learn something from it and move on. This part is not about quick fixes, it's the long and painful stuff that if we push through, can give us real breakthroughs.

WHAT AM I THINKING?

When we notice a negative feeling, it's usually due to a negative thought. These thoughts are automatic, usually unnoticed by us as they lurk in the background beaming out bad vibes – but we have to learn to catch the moment we start to feel bad and ask ourselves, what did I think that made me feel this way?

We all like to believe we're in total control, but we're mostly on autopilot. I assume you're not consciously pumping your heart as you read this? Even if we're actively considering our mental health, there's only so much of our mind that is apparent on the surface. Most of our brain activity happens as a background process that distantly dictates how we feel. If we hit the ctrl+alt+del of our minds, we might be shocked to see what's taking up all the memory and processing power. That recurring thought loop about the awkward moment you had telling that person working at the cinema to 'enjoy the film too'? We need to end that task because your mentalhealth.exe is not responding.

CHANGING YOUR MIND

Our brains have a reassuring power called 'neuroplasticity' – basically meaning they constantly change and learn. There are billions upon billions of neurons in your mind, forming the connections that make up your consciousness. Scientists used to believe that our brains stop developing as we progress through life, but in recent decades we've discovered that our brains form new connections over time as we adapt to our environment and experiences. What this means for our mental health is that we are really not fixed in stone. We have the power to rewire our minds to rise to challenges and grow past our old, unhelpful habits. Even if we have adverse experiences, we can adapt and change. All it takes is a conscious effort to start, and keep up the progress. The power is in our hands.

Our minds are in a constant state of alert (potentially stressful, but it is trying to be helpful) and tend to fall back on what we've learned from past incidents. The trouble is that every situation in life may not be as intense as the particularly bad incident your brain learned a lesson from, so when your mind recognises a situation and fires off the first response to keep you safe, it may be a totally inappropriate overreaction. Before you know it, you're crying in the club because your brain was subconsciously reminded of that time a clown sprayed water in your face when you were a toddler. We need to break free from these base responses to try to see the truth of what's happening in the present and question if we really need to think or feel this way.

These responses are called **thinking biases**, and all of us are probably prone to most of these at some point. Once you learn to recognise them and back away from them, it can really take the heat out of negative feelings. If you relate to every one of these – congratulations, you win! ... the prize of really having to dedicate your energy to stopping your mind from spiralling you into oblivion. Good luck, everyone. In practice, it shouldn't be too hard to beat.

EMOTIONAL REASONING

Remember Sandra and her stupid lottery ticket? Just because you start to 'feel' bad about something doesn't mean you have evidence that the situation is as bad or stressful as you feel.

- You **feel** jealous, so you assume your partner is definitely cheating on you.
- You **feel** anxious before an event, so convince yourself that something bad is going to happen there.
- You **feel** like no one likes you, so you believe it's fundamentally true and avoid seeing a friend altogether.

We need to separate the feeling from the thinking. Step back and look at the facts. Is the thing you are worrying about really going to happen? How likely is it? What else could happen? How would you view the situation if you 'felt' good? Don't let your fearful or pessimistic reactions hold you back. Recognise the feeling as a protective signal from your brain – then push past it to see the truth.

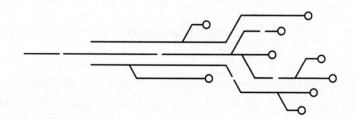

MIND READING

／

We're probably not psychic, but we all act like we must be sometimes. It's our brains' self-protective nature to assume the worst in others in case they hurt us. The truth is that we mostly do not know what other people are thinking or what they will do, we're just prophesying our own doom to try to protect ourselves. If we judge someone before speaking to them, misread social cues, or have an agenda to avoid a situation, we can convince ourselves of something with no proof.

The next time you feel 'they think I'm annoying', 'he doesn't want to see me', 'she doesn't want me on the team' – ask yourself what real evidence you have of this? If someone hasn't responded to your message and you just have a bad feeling that they hate you, you're probably wrong. If several people have come to you and said that João lost his phone in a horrifying tricycle incident, you have something real to reassure you.

• 'She doesn't want me on the team.' → Actually she asked me how I feel about the try outs, because she must be considering me.

CATASTROPHISING

／

Yes, my favourite. When you are worried about something, so you run away with these feelings and spend all day imagining the worst, most disastrous thing that could possibly happen. It's totally giving in to your negative feelings and letting them take you on a wild ride of doom and gloom. If you make one small mistake, you may convince yourself that instead of being able to fix it in any way, it's an irrevocable disaster, everyone hates you, your life is over as you know it and the only reasonable solution is to stow away on a cargo boat to the mid-Pacific and join a pod of dolphins.

Ask yourself what all the outcomes are – not just the worst scenario, but the best, and what is actually likely, given the things that you can control. You can probably just mop up the drink you spilled, you didn't ruin the bar mitzvah. The bigger the picture you try to see, the less all-consumed with worry you will feel.

- 'If I don't get there on time my life is *literally* over.' → There's several things I can do to get there faster, it's okay to be a bit late, even if I am I will be fine.

ALL-OR-NOTHING THINKING

Following on from focusing on the worst outcome with catastrophising, we need to appreciate that life doesn't just exist in the extremes. As a chronic perfectionist, I tend to imagine a 'perfect' outcome to something, and the only other possibility is the catastrophic destruction scenario. More than just being unhelpful to imagine the worst case, it's unhealthy to hold yourself to a standard where things are either perfect, or an automatic failure. We need to manage our expectations in life to be content with the middle-ground, as too much pressure can make us crumble. My perfectionism does have the bonus of keeping me motivated and covering my back (by perpetually hypothetically worrying about everything that can go wrong) but it's stressful, moment-to-moment, and can wear you down in the long run. We aren't all amazing at everything. Your worth as a person isn't based on what you achieve. Relax your rules for the world and yourself.

- 'If my book isn't a bestseller it's completely worthless.' → If just one person reads my book and feels like they've learned how to make themselves happier, I have done a good thing. I hope they are having an okay day.'

MENTAL FILTERING

It's like selective vision for your mind. One of the most profound realisations I've had about humanity in general is that we often focus on the negatives – which sounds quite distressing, but implies that in life there are enough positives for us to not find interesting, which is reassuring. Depending on our outlook on life, we have a baseline expectation and if anything shocking suddenly pops up, that's naturally more interesting than regular life. The trouble is, if we spend too much time focusing on one small negative thing when the big picture is actually fine, our whole experience will be dragged down.

A relatable example in modern life is seeing something mean on the internet. We could spend all day reading posts from interesting people, looking at nice photos of our friends and laughing at the things we seek out to make us feel better.

But then if among a day's browsing you were to suddenly stumble upon one salty comment from a particularly pissed off person who's trying hard to poop in the punch bowl, it tends to be the thing that sticks in your mind. We have to remind ourselves that life isn't going to be totally perfect; there will be bad moments. Even then, we need to look at the bad moment and instead of feeling shocked and hurt that it existed, break it down and try to understand it. Did that person even mean what they said, or are they just having a bad day? Are they lost and confused? Is their message going to really harm anything other than your mood? Most importantly: is this one negative thing in your day worth focusing all your emotional time and energy on? Probably not. Accept that life isn't incident-less, try to see the bigger context around it, and don't let it define your day. Look up and appreciate the amount of good stuff you aren't taking as much time to acknowledge. How's the big picture? Probably fine.

- 'A customer left a one-star review of my food.' → That one customer read the sign wrong and didn't know the difference between a macaron and a macaroon. They also said it 'tasted like nightmares' which clearly isn't serious. Also they tripped over while leaving the shop so were probably mainly just embarrassed. Also a hundred other people said they had the best cake of their life. It was actually a very rewarding day running my popup ferret café.

PERSONALISATION

/

When we're in the mood for some moping, we're inherently talented at taking total responsibility for something bad happening, even if it was not in our control. If we're only a part of something, or couldn't reasonably have changed what happened, it's not fair to put all of the burden or shame on our shoulders. It's not about letting yourself off the hook (which if you do too much, you've got a whole other kind of problem), it's just not punishing yourself for things outside of your control.

A common example that I experienced is your parents fighting when you are a child and deciding to blame yourself for their falling out – but not realising that they need to take accountability for their own actions. Ask yourself if you are really responsible, and what else could have been done, and how much of that was really up to you.

• 'I missed their cat's birthday party and I've let them down.' →
  Actually they gave me the wrong address, the car broke down,
  a family of geese closed the road for ten hours and there was a
  tornado, so it's not totally my fault.

OVERGENERALISING

/

In an effort to make things simple, we take one thing happening once and decide to save time by applying that to everything that ever happens. These thoughts often include phrases like 'always' and 'never'. If scientists saw something happen once and concluded as though it was always the case, we'd be living in a dangerous, highly explosive and probably contagious world. You need to do the same with your feelings – just because it happened once, doesn't mean it will happen the exact same way again. It's a shortcut way of thinking, that usually comes from a place of fear of confronting the challenge, but unless we rise to it we may never know the truth.

If you have one bad date, it doesn't mean you need to search for the nearest castle tower and lock yourself in it. Make yourself work a bit harder and dig deeper – what was specific to this disaster-date that probably won't happen again? What things could you have changed? As always, separate how you first feel from thinking about what is the truth.

• 'I lost one football match, I will never win again.' → They were actually the best team in the entire world so it's not realistic that I would have won, also I will remember to wear shoes next time.

When we apply this 'generalising' way of thinking to another person, that's when we fall into another basic human behaviour: labelling. If you find yourself thinking things like 'they're selfish' or 'they're always late', consider if you have enough evidence to make that true, or if you're taking one incident and projecting that onto their entire existence. It may not be fair to prematurely label someone this way, and you may even miss out on a relationship if you close the door.

It's very likely that at least some of these thinking biases play out regularly in your mind, after all your mind is just trying to protect you from threats, like an extremely eager dog attacking your neighbours. Sometimes, you just need to let the mail man deliver the envelope. There's no need to bite.

We tend to have a few signature thinking biases we're mainly guilty of, depending on our psychological makeup. You may have recognised some in that list, and now you can start to appreciate how they are unhelpful and try to rise above. When left unchecked, they can really wear us down, make us more stressed than we really need to be, and take the kind of long-term toll on our mental health that can lead us on a path to self-doubt, depression and anxiety. The first time I questioned my thinking this way, it immediately made me feel better and less pressured by the feeling that popped into my mind. If we can master this skill of noticing our thoughts and questioning them, we will be in a better place to look after ourselves going forward in life, thinking rationally and feeling in control.

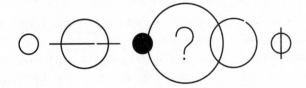

EXERCISE: CHALLENGING YOUR THOUGHTS

Good for:
- Taking the heat out of negative feelings
- Getting perspective
- Looking after your long-term mental health

1. Notice a negative feeling and find the thought behind it
2. Describe what you're thinking
3. See what evidence you have to back up that thought
4. Consider any thinking biases that are clouding your judgement
5. Try to see a more reasonable way of looking at the situation
6. Put this in perspective to see what's really at stake
7. Reconsider what you think and how you feel about it

Situation	She didn't reply to my text
Emotion	Sad/lonely/angry
Thought	She hates me/She thinks I'm boring
Evidence that supports the thought	She's done this before. She yawned a lot last time we were together.
Evidence that doesn't support the thought	She usually replies to my messages – this is just 1 message out of 100s. I'm just mind reading/catastrophising.
Alternative view	She is very busy working late, so probably just hasn't seen the message.
Outcome	Less sad, lonely and angry. Chill out and wait for a reply, make some pasta.

RULES AND REGULATIONS

As we learn from the world around us, our mistakes and interactions with other people, we build up a set of beliefs and ideas for how we think the world works and the expectations we have for humanity.

We all adopt our own set of rules – like a silent guidebook each of us has for getting through life, which we believe will keep us safe in the face of negativity. So if you believe you're unlovable, you might have a rule about not letting anyone see the 'real you', or if you believe that others are cruel, you might have a rule in your mind about keeping everyone at arm's length to protect yourself.

These rules in our mind define how we behave, react to situations, and how we think and feel about what happens to us. If from our life experience we believe that people are trustworthy and kind, then we may have a sunnier outlook on life, but could be substantially hurt the first time we are let down. Conversely, if we *expect* people to be unhelpful and unreliable, we may be better at protecting ourselves from betrayal, but we distance ourselves from intimacy that could bring us joy. Our aim should be to second-guess our nature and be open to new experiences that change our outlook!

These rules within us can be a helpful way to shortcut how to deal with a situation, to save effort, or protect us from harm – but if we're not flexible they can hold us back and keep us feeling down. The trouble is when they're extreme, with absolutes like *always, never, must* and *should*. If, for whatever reason, you go through life thinking 'I must never make mistakes' or 'I must always make people like me' you are inevitably putting too much pressure on yourself and setting unreachable goals.

If we have fundamental views of ourselves, when we're feeling low, such as we are 'defective', this is not true, it's just how you may have been taught to believe. The danger is that when we act according to these beliefs, and follow the rules that these beliefs have shaped, we tend to get results that make us believe them even more strongly. Basically, fuelling the fire of internal hatred. Sounds dramatic, because it is actually super-dramatic.

It should be all of our missions, in more ways than just mental health (such as prejudices we hold or things we are ignorant about), to surpass our default programming, learn, grow and become an honest and happy version of us, for ourselves and others.

EXPOSING YOURSELF

A common rule affecting our behaviour is our relationship with vulnerability. To have good mental health it's important to be able to tell people how you feel, to ask for help if you need it, and to understand that it's perfectly normal and not something to feel shame about. The problem is that our natural survival instinct is to project strength and reject outside interference in case we are in danger.

All of us feel a pressure to appear as if we're coping and happy. How often do we answer the casual question 'How are you?' with total honesty? Granted it might be a bit too much info to give the sixteen-year-old handing you a pizza on a freezing road, but it's the truth.

As a British guy, the 'stiff upper lip' mentality of trying to just keep calm and carry on is prevalent in the society I grew up in and exist in today. Thinking to the start of this journey, where we discussed how priorities can push mental wellbeing to the background, hiding vulnerability can be a useful tool to get us through extreme situations. I learned behaviours from my dad, and he learned them from his Royal Air Force pilot father before him – the attitude my grandfather adopted to survive was passed down to generations that didn't necessarily need it.

World War II left a profound scar in the culture of the UK, mainly from the efforts of the soldiers who sacrificed their lives to fight, and the people at home who toiled and persevered to support them and survive. When you are in such an extreme environment, it makes sense to engage this 'stiff upper lip' attitude in order to persevere – however, it's not sustainable for the duration of a whole of a human life, as the toll it takes on you mentally and physically will come back for a piece later.

Whilst the hostilities I've encountered in life are admittedly not as immediately dangerous as an anti-aircraft cannon, I inherited that mindset. It served me well to protect myself against violence from other kids, by projecting a strong exterior image and never giving an emotional reaction – but as an adult I realised the damage it inflicted as I felt alone, unsupported and generally resentful towards society for making me suffer in silence. This definitely contributed to how I felt, and my view of the world, when I had my darkest moment. We all may need to keep our heads down in times of adversity, but we need to understand that it should only be a temporary solution and definitely not an aspirational mindset for life.

Glamorising this mindset when it is not necessary is fundamentally damaging. The idea of a person with a hard exoskeleton, that doesn't complain, doesn't need to ask for help and projects immovable strength is great for collective perseverance and intimidating the enemy – but unless you are in a situation that requires this extreme mentality, the only enemy may be yourself. We can respect the strength of people who faced adversity before us, without fetishising their struggle when we aren't going through it ourselves, because it only makes us perform worse!

DON'T YOU KNOW THAT YOU'RE TOXIC?

When I was growing up, my father was a stereotypical 'macho man', who insisted on acting strong and in control all of his life. He was incredibly proud and took great offence at anything that questioned his ability. The issue is that he, like all of us, was not always right, winning, or okay. I saw first-hand how embarrassed he was to not be as physically capable as he had been when he was younger, to ask for help in even the mildest of scenarios – if he burst a tyre on the car, or even to tell me how he was really feeling – instead of projecting the image of the head of the family. As time has passed, I look back with pity to see a person who was clearly struggling in so many ways, but it was his struggle with shame that held him back from facing his issues in life.

It's understandable that humans generally don't like criticism, especially if people imply that just by behaving how we've been taught all our lives, we're suddenly doing something wrong, and are immediately expected to change. It can feel like we're being punished, without necessarily intending any harm – which often results in a push-back, even if we now understand how our behaviour can be harmful. 'Toxic masculinity' is definitely a phrase which lots of men feel defensive about hearing, probably because – as with my dad – if they are struggling with their mental health for any reason related to the 'pressures' of stereotypical male roles in society (that they likely didn't choose), never having felt they can ask for help, they resent being at fault.

What men need to realise is that in a 'patriarchal' society, they are also the victims of gender roles which tell them to ignore their mental health. Suicide is the one of the main causes of death for young men. People have been raised by their families, and our culture, to reject vulnerability. Archaic stereotypes of men having to be physically strong, or to carry the financial burden of a family without complaint, lead to an inevitable crumble under the pressure if there's no release. Teaching that 'boys don't cry' doesn't work. If they aren't allowed to cry, they might give up and die. I'm the first radical in the queue to demolish gender roles in our society, but the good news for the concerned traditional man reading is: don't feel attacked – this is an opportunity to set yourself free. If you join in the demolition, you can continue to live your life, but with the added bonus of honesty, support, and better mental health.

I used 'masculinity' as a personal example that has affected me, but analyse your own identity, culture and story and ask yourself if there are any stereotypes or societal pressures that are holding you back for no damn reason. Stop holding it in. Let the dam break.

Having the
bravery and honesty
to admit what is
wrong and ask for
help is strength.

LET IT SNOW

Even recently, the term 'snowflakes' (a big red flag for a typically brain-numbingly depressing and pointless debate incoming) has risen in popularity to describe mainly young people being open about vulnerability. I completely reject the idea of this term, as attempting to hide your vulnerability is clearly a sign of fear (which, as a long time closet-dweller, I understand). Having the bravery and honesty to admit what is wrong and ask for help is strength. Not only does it show you can defeat your fear to rise above your brain's basic instinct, but you will become a better and more powerful person when you overcome your adversity.

If young people today are embracing this attitude towards their own vulnerability, I think the future of our society will be more prosperous and fundamentally happier. The hardest part is if you are someone who feels attacked by this notion, as you have spent your life buried by the burden of these rules. Give yourself permission, at any point, to drop the self-imposed shackles and the shame that comes with them. You are not a fool, it may not be your fault, and you have not wasted your time. You have nothing to lose by changing your mindset to something that makes you happier. It's hard, but I did it in the face of all the homophobic hate I experienced, and believe me there was a lot of baggage to sort out. I feel very silly for all the time I wasted projecting a false image of impenetrability whilst quietly trembling behind it, but being afraid to admit fault and 'look a bit silly' is a completely stupid reason to avoid living a healthier and happier life.

No matter what it was that may have taught you to close yourself off from help – if you want to feel better and be better, accept your vulnerability, accept your weaknesses, and with honesty you can start to heal.

BREAKING THE RULES

So you want to surpass your default programming? Congratulations, being aware of the simulation is the first step. Now for the analysis.

Think about the different areas of your life: work, relationships, family. Ask yourself what rules you hold yourself accountable to. What kind of things do you accept or not tolerate?

Do any of these 'if, then' rules resonate with you?

• 'If I don't always . . . . then this will happen: . . . .'
(e.g. 'If I don't always achieve top marks, people will know I'm stupid')

• 'I must always . . . . or else . . . .'
(e.g. 'I must always make people laugh, or else they'll leave me')

• 'I must never . . . . to protect me from . . . .'
('I must never admit I'm a furry, to protect me from cyberbullying')

Are these rules good for you, or unhealthy? Consider if they are unrealistic or unfair to yourself, and setting you up to be stressed, or have other negative consequences.

You might already have a sense of what fear your 'rules' are trying to protect you from being hurt by, but don't worry about changing them overnight (they may have been learned over your lifetime!), just be aware of them so you have the power to question your thinking.

Rather than trying to change overnight, consider just making them fairer:

- 'I must always be the best.' → 'I'll try to do my best but it's okay not to always be at the top.'

- 'I must never let anyone see the real me.' → 'It's okay to be myself, even if not everybody likes me.'

Feel free to fail. If you're challenging your outlook on life to try to be happier overall, it's okay to experiment, even if it ends up being worse. Sometimes you can only know if your preconceived notions are holding you back by taking a leap of faith. I believe.

EXERCISE: EXPERIMENTING WITH YOUR THOUGHTS

Good for:
- **Overcoming mental barriers**
- **Learning about yourself**
- **Facing your fears**

Mental barriers can feel a lot harder to overcome than physical ones. If you see something you have to climb over, at least you understand what is required. Sometimes the mental problems in our lives are difficult to define, and can hold us back from accomplishing so much.

You can attempt a 'behavioural experiment' which lets you get distance from your raw feelings, to try to look at yourself like a scientist. Come up with a prediction, see if it's true – then decide if those thoughts and feelings are worth paying attention to.

1. Choose something you're worried about, or a situation you think may go wrong. This could be an event, a piece of work or a social interaction.
2. Make a clear note of what you're afraid will happen.
3. Rate how likely you think it is that this will really happen. If it's not 100%, there's already a possibility it could go better than you think!
4. Test your prediction by doing the thing. Once you've done it, come back to your note and consider if it was really as bad, in hindsight, as you thought it would be. What people tend to find is that their predictions were way off, and either you were completely wrong, or at least seemingly a lot less bothered than you thought you'd be!

Of course, don't experiment with anything too dangerous or important in your life, but whatever you may do, remember it's okay to fail, because you're trying to learn about yourself and grow. Blame science.

DAN'S FANTASY EXPERIMENT

Thought or belief	I'm painfully socially awkward and I will embarrass myself at this event. Likelihood: 99%
Experiment	Introduce myself to a total stranger at the hotel bar this weekend.
Prediction	I will say something really strange and they will walk away silently while rolling their eyes. Likelihood: 98.9%
Outcome – what actually happened?	I said something strange, but he laughed. It was an accidental icebreaker, we're now running away to get secretly married.
Learning – how does the outcome fit your original belief?	Perhaps I was awkward, but there was no reason to be so afraid of it. Next time I'll try to talk to more people, and I'll try not to worry in advance. Worth the experiment!

LESS STRESS

Stress is probably, unless you live on a beach doing... not much, a somewhat regular presence in your life. We feel stressed when a situation demands more of us than what we consider our ability to cope. It is sent to us as a signal, warning us to get out of the situation or to rest.

Each of us tolerates a different amount of stress. Some of us thrive on it and seem to live constantly on the edge of disaster, where stress is almost a symbiotic motivator used as a tool to push us over the line and keep our senses heightened. For others, stress can be quickly exhausting and too much of it can take a real toll on our physical and mental health. Life isn't a competition to see how cool you are by handling the most stress at any moment until you explode. (Nothing aspirational about fainting while sprinting around an office.) It's about balancing an amount that is right for us. 'Acute' stress is likely to appear for a brief moment during a situation in our lives. 'Chronic' stress comes from a lifestyle or environment that keeps you constantly feeling this way, and can be seriously detrimental.

We aren't meant to be perpetually stressed, it's like an alarm going off constantly – if we ignore it for too long, there's a big and potentially flaming issue that is about to become a problem for us. The good news is that stress can be managed. As a reaction to what's going on around you, it's more in your control than some of the deeper emotional issues that are more difficult to diagnose. Managing stress is a project for you throughout life. Measure the levels of it and try not to have too much of it for too long.

Acute – short-term, in-the-moment stress (shit, I just realised I forgot my house keys / I've got too much to do today)

Chronic – long-term stress that sticks around, particularly if you're always exposed to the problem (ongoing financial problems, toxic environments / discrimination)

Assess the stressor

Stressors are the things that cause stress, in case you didn't guess. These things include situations that change our regular way of doing things, that bring increased scrutiny from other people – but can also be things that should be considered 'good', like moving house, getting married, or starting a new job. Though if your wedding is more than just moderately stressful, and you've postponed the big day eleven times, it might be a red flag. Run.

THE STRESS BUCKET

The best way to visualise the balance between 'stress' and 'coping' is to imagine the bucket of your mind filling up with the bubbling liquid of stress. When the bucket overflows, it starts to leak into the other aspects of your life – losing sleep, losing patience, all the way up to losing hair. You need to manage this level by metaphorically turning off the stress tap (by stopping the demands taking up your life) or put a hole in the bottom of the bucket (by doing a stress-relieving activity). It's another example of being proactive about your mental health – don't wait until you suddenly snap; try to notice when you are feeling too stressed and intervene by slowing down or taking time out to keep your levels in check.

If you're going through a difficult time, your ability to cope with stressful situations will be compromised. You may even struggle to handle the day-to-day things you usually have no trouble with. Keep in mind that during challenging times, you may need to be extra-proactive about your stress levels!

Stressors don't have to be single events – they can be the pile-up of daily hassles that take up your brain-space until you can't handle any more. It's true that one bad day can tip you over the edge, if it begins with burnt toast and ends with a rogue mouse biting your nipple as you try to sleep.

Assess your life right now. What is currently demanding things of you? What's putting you under extra pressure or challenge? Are there parts of your daily life that stress you out too much? Once you identify what these things are, you can start to mitigate them.

STRESSFUL SYMPTOMS

How do you know when you're stressed? For most of us, we know. We just know. If I asked you to describe it, however, you may have trouble particularly articulating exactly what it is? The symptoms of stress fall into three areas with some classic signs you may experience at different points:

Physical – headaches, fatigue, sleep problems, tense muscles, aching joints, digestive problems, palpitations, and changing appetite / weight / sex drive.

Emotional – easily irritable, flustered, overwhelmed, demotivated, depressed, anxious.

Behavioural – overeating / not eating enough, overworking, avoiding socialising, trouble concentrating, difficulty making decisions, forgetfulness, turning to substances like alcohol or drugs.

When I was doing my show on live radio, I really lost perspective on how unreasonably unhelped I was, how stressful it was, and the toll it took on me. Hearing the news that we got the gig two weeks before the first show set us up for a whirlwind ride, and my own creative ambition made what I wanted to achieve with it almost impossible. Sitting on the last train home on the London Underground, I probably experienced every single symptom written above at once. What I wish I could have read, instead of the news from a discarded paper with a business man's butt imprint crinkled deeply into the pages, is that I should recognise when I'm stressed and there are many ways to cope with it.

Coping styles

'Coping' with stress means finding balance between the pressures coming into your life and how you manage it. For times in life when you know you're stressed, there are two broad approaches to coping with it.

PROBLEM-FOCUSED COPING:
FOR WHEN THERE IS A SOLUTION WITHIN YOUR CONTROL

This is taking a proactive and practical approach to removing stress or minimising how much gets put on you – doing this can help you be more resilient in stressful situations going forward.

Try to reduce the demands on you by problem-solving solutions, asking for help, or removing the things that are causing stress.

- If you have too much work: prioritise your time, consult your colleagues, ask for an extension, or run away to live in a remote wood cabin in Alaska and befriend some beavers.

- If you have a noisy neighbour: ask them to be quiet, write a passive aggressive letter, call the police, install soundproofing walls in your house, murder them.

Okay, there are different levels of intensity you can approach problem solving with – just go for the nice, middle-ground ones that work for you and won't start an FBI manhunt.

PROBLEM-FOCUSED COPING FOR STRESS

- What can I do to minimise or manage my stress?

- Are there things that I'm avoiding that I could try to deal with?

- What personal strengths can I harness here?

- How have I dealt with similar situations in the past?

- How can I break things down into smaller, manageable steps?

- Can I bring in anyone else to help me?

EMOTION-FOCUSED COPING:
FOR WHEN THE SITUATION IS OUT OF YOUR CONTROL

When you can't control the thing causing you stress, you can try to distance yourself from it and reduce the emotional pressure it puts on you. This can also mean allowing yourself time to relax and recharge – which may not have solved the problem, but gives you the energy to tackle it.

When choosing a way to cope with your emotions, you should be sure that it is a 'healthy' behaviour that will set you up to return to handle what was causing you stress. If you take time away to socialise with friends, sit in sunshine, or read a book, you will hopefully be harmlessly relaxing (if you're reading this while skateboarding down the side of a volcano, okay I guess). If you lean too heavily on 'unhealthy' things like drugs and alcohol, they can provide a quick fix but will ultimately make you feel worse in the long term. Make sure, when you are choosing how to make yourself feel better, that you go in fully knowing the consequences, and aren't just thinking about how you're feeling now, but how you will feel later and if that will help you recover enough to rise back to the stressful challenge.

It's also important not to suppress the emotion, as trying to hide your emotions is just another stressful thing that can eat away at you and keep you from finding a real solution. Tackle the stressors in your life when you can – before it's too late and it piles up. If it's something out of your control, cope with the emotions by taking time away and doing things to help you relax and recover.

You can manage the physical symptoms with movement, good nutrition, getting good sleep and practicing your mindful mental health techniques. Practicing slow breathing can calm down the body in-the-moment so you can focus your mind on solving the problem or addressing your emotions.

Just remember that stress is normal and can be useful, but we should never let it simmer relentlessly in the background. As with everything else so far, learning to notice how you feel and intervene, recognising what you can and can't control, and managing how you feel as you go, are all key to maintaining healthy stress levels in the long term. By all means, feel free to go on a pizza binge and drink a crate of beer, it will distract you temporarily – as long as you accept the reality-shattering headache that awaits you. Otherwise, just breathe.

EMOTION-FOCUSED COPING FOR STRESS

- Am I accepting my feelings or trying to push them away?

- Am I criticising myself for the way I'm feeling?

- Who can I lean on for support?

- Do I need to take time away from what is causing me stress?

- What can I do to relieve stress and help me recover?

- How can I prioritise self-care right now?

ELEPHANTS AND SKELETONS

For some of us, getting to the root of our emotional issues and relationship with mental health is about more than what you can control now.

As much as you can know how to be mindful and present, how to improve your daily life and environment – and even assess your mindset and manage emotions going forward – there may be a bigger issue pulling you down. Maybe there is something you're carrying from the past that influences how you see yourself now? Or you've noticed repeating past patterns and behaviours in your current relationships? A part of your life story that you haven't come to terms with yet? This may be a trauma.

Psychologists are increasingly paying attention to the lasting impact that trauma can have on mental health. The trauma might include a major one-time incident, like an accident or natural disaster – but traumas can also be subtle, or prolonged: things like toxic relationships, financial stress, neglectful parenting, or bullying. When we experience a trauma, our brain often struggles to make sense of what happened. Traumatic events can shatter our beliefs about the world, humanity, or our confidence, making it hard to just sweep them under the rug and press forward.

Because traumatic events can be so hard to think about, our brains may not process the memories in the same way as non-traumatic memories. It's as if everything in your brain is neatly categorised, with things from your favourite sitcom quotes or your PIN code ready to recall when you need it (now I've mentioned your PIN, you will forget it the next time you need to use it, sorry), but traumatic memories refuse to slot into their file, and keep popping up randomly when you don't want them to.

Traumas often shatter our beliefs about the world, humanity, or our own vulnerability, so we often can't just sweep them under the carpet and move on.

Trigger happy

For all of us, certain things will 'trigger' upsetting memories or emotions. Triggers aren't always obvious, and could include things like the honk of a horn reminding you of a car crash, a smell or song bringing back a memory of a bad day, or even someone's actions reminding you of the way that someone else treated you in the past. When you experience a flashback, you can have the same intense feelings that you had at the time of the trauma, often accompanied by vivid images of what happened as you suddenly remember.

If you realise that casual reminders can trigger old memories, their associated feelings, or you feel like your emotional reaction is definitely disproportionate to the situation, it can be a sign that there is something unresolved that you need to address.

It's understandable that we should be aware and compassionate of this in others, especially if we ever control what other people see or experience. This is why 'content warnings' can be helpful if a specific issue may be present. It's safe to say this book has touched upon several topics which, depending on where someone's at or their experiences in life, they may not be ready or able to read about – which is why we placed a note in the opening pages. The same logic applies to 'safe spaces' for people who may really need them, to feel they can relax without a looming threat. It is not a ridiculous concept, as some suggest, that is catering too heavily to vulnerabilities – some people really need it.

Experiencing trauma doesn't always lead to full-blown PTSD (post-traumatic stress disorder) – where you feel jumpy and overly alert to danger, often experiencing flashbacks or nightmares; it can be much more subtle, simply leaving you with a sense of vulnerability, shame, or feeling like you're haunted by something that you can't quite pin down.

Stuck in the cupboard

If you have gone through a long struggle, stemming from your upbringing or identity, these experiences over time can leave wounds, that if not confronted or healed, can keep us trapped in the past or constantly pulled back to a vulnerable state. If you find yourself being tormented by events earlier in your life, or that despite everything you've tried, you are still feeling bad, it may be time to look deeper, further back, and perhaps consider getting professional help.

Life is hectic and busy and the default state for most of us is to relentlessly push forward. We can feel compelled to try to ignore difficult things in our past, as we probably have so many issues we have to deal with right now, and are more focused on achieving things for our future. The problem is that the past catches up with us whenever we are vulnerable, so you may be able to keep the momentum going for a while, but none of us should live with the feeling that we're being chased.

Through my twenties, I had that feeling of momentum. Everything was focused on escaping my environment, building a life for myself, and trying to secure freedom on my own terms – financially and emotionally. I was always aware that I had some vague 'baggage', but definitely didn't have the time, energy, or even the will to dwell on it. I had a mission to accomplish. The reality was that the way that I had been treated as a young person was not normal or acceptable. I learned to tolerate abuse in order to survive, and the relentless messages that I was inferior or invalid seeped into me, making me profoundly sad and insecure. I developed an incredibly paranoid and cynical world view – which served me well in ways, as everything I achieved went through such a layer of scrutiny and criticism from myself, that anything I gave to the world was as perfectly rounded as I could possibly make it. This took its toll on me by making me constantly exhausted, physically and emotionally. I became that perfectionist with impossible standards, who was an incredible procrastinator because of the level of fear I built up for everything in life.

I defined my entire worth not around my happiness, or how full my world was in all the ways I could enjoy – but purely based on how I was perceived by others, and the visible 'success' of my life and career. I wasn't prioritising my actual feelings, but numbers and praise. I couldn't stop running, couldn't stop climbing up, because I knew there was something standing over my shoulder,

None of us should live with the feeling that we're being chased.

and would just go back to being at the mercy of other people again. It was only in moments where I recognised my mental health was not normal, and I may have been struggling from depression, or when I decided that I had to confront my sexuality and the reality of how I had been treated when younger, that I finally started to feel relief. Tackling these things was an intimidating and incredibly difficult journey to begin, one that I'm definitely not done with yet, but it was absolutely necessary in order to improve my mental health and be happy.

Coming to terms

The beginning of this journey for you may be to simply come to terms with what you've been through. I always knew I was some kind of not-straight, but there is a difference between it being a vague, ominous feeling in the background, and fully acknowledging and accepting it. Depending on your circumstance, there may be something you have to resolve, or something you have to confront, but what's important is to protect ourselves. If you feel like it's something you can't handle alone, reach out to someone you trust. If you feel like it is potentially upsetting or dangerous, working through it with a doctor or therapist may be necessary.

Traumatic incidents, or general adversity in life, can develop into clinical depression or anxiety disorders, which need serious help to shift. Problems like these may sound very dramatic on paper, but actually one in four adults experiences a mental health problem in any given year, and the good news is that there are many approaches to treatment, so getting help is the right thing to do. The sooner you reach out, the better. Hopefully you know if the problem is something that just needs another person's support, and you know someone who you can trust with something so intimate. If you need more professional help, we all need to know how to access that if or when we need it.

It can feel very serious and heavy to consider reaching out to a professional about your mental health. You are likely to feel fear of the unknown about what you may experience or discover, and possibly shame about admitting vulnerability, or of being judged by people who find out. The reality is, with the fears and mental health struggles, these problems are so common that it's much more exciting in your head than it really is.

Remember that professionals' entire careers are based around hearing people's stories and helping – so trust me, as someone who has consulted a dozen doctors and more than a handful of therapists (with all the fear each time) they have seen and heard everything before, and they are there to help you. You can call ahead, write a letter or an email, slide a note under the door, even get a friend to help you talk to them if you need it! Whatever gets you in that door to get help.

LEAVE IT
TO THE PROS

If you feel like you need more help with your mental health, speaking to a doctor or therapist can seem daunting, but there's nothing to be afraid of.

Therapy

I won't lie, when I first saw a therapist I was disappointed.
Not with the experience – that was profound and arguably life
changing; I mean the room. I was not sitting in some grand
library study, reclining on a chaise longue while a man with a
floor-length beard hummed every time I spoke. The room was
concrete. The man was a nice woman. It was also a lot more
casual, calm, and probably more helpful than anything I'd seen
or heard in a story.

The goal of therapy is for a professional to talk you through
your problems. It will typically begin with an 'assessment', which
may feel like a casual icebreaking conversation, for the therapist
to understand your life, your current situation, and what you
need help with. They are trained to help you make sense of how
you feel, understand what you want from therapy (and what you
want to achieve), sometimes reflect on the past, and help you to
move forward.

There are many different approaches and a good therapist will get
to know you and explore the best way of working with you to feel
better. It's likely they will help you to understand your negative
thoughts and feelings, to find the origin of any issues that are
blocking your progress, and put things in perspective so you feel
you can start to tackle your problems.

One of the most profound parts of therapy is realising that the
simple act of talking to and sharing how you honestly feel with

a person can be the most helpful way to lift yourself out of a situation you may feel stuck in. If we feel we can trust a professional, who is not only bound by their qualifications and integrity to keep our conversations confidential, but is also trained to know the best way to protect us and manage our emotions, we can open up about things we may have never felt safe enough to before.

NOT ALL HEAVY

Therapy isn't just for people dealing with intense issues around trauma – it can help anyone! Even if you feel you are generally slightly too anxious, stressed, or can't deal with a small problem in your life, the power of having someone to talk to, giving qualified advice, is immense. If we lived in a world where it was affordable and accessible to everyone, I would honestly force everyone to do it, like a benevolent mental health dictator. Society would be profoundly transformed overnight if people were obliged to share their feelings in a trusting environment and be encouraged to think about their minds and solve their problems.

There is no right or wrong reason to go to therapy, it's not about being worthy or unwell enough – any effort to make yourself feel better is commendable.

Even if you may not be able (or want) to see a therapist, recognise that simply sharing your problems and feelings with others, and involving other people in the process of helping yourself, is a great way to tackle your problems in life.

Sharing how you honestly feel with a person can be the most helpful way to lift yourself out of a situation you may feel stuck in.

The truth is that many of us have the power to help ourselves and each other, we just may not know how, or be too afraid of the risks. Therapy is a way to give you a safe environment, with the right person to take you through whatever issues you feel you need help with.

When it comes to trauma, no matter what approach the therapist takes, they'll be committed to helping you to make sense of it, and process the emotions associated with it. Although thinking about trauma is not easy, when therapy helps you through that it can be a real game-changer and many people walk away feeling like a huge weight has lifted. It's about safely acknowledging it, learning about it, and if not resolving it then at least learning how to live with it in a way you can manage, instead of feeling constantly troubled by it on your own.

FINDING THE ONE

As with any relationship in life, the success of it will depend on your compatibility with that person. People spend their whole lives searching for their best friend, artists seek their most productive creative partner, sports personalities quest for their dream physio. It's the same with therapists. You aren't looking for a friend to laugh around with, though that might make it easier – it's about who you feel you can trust, and whose energy you feel encourages you to share the things you find difficult to say. I have tried several therapists in my life and it took a few before I found a situation I felt was sustainable. Some people were too sympathetic, too serious, or just seemed confused – but I knew I couldn't be discouraged, and it was worth persisting to have that supportive presence in my life.

The other important factor is to make sure they're registered with a professional body and have the qualifications. Just because your aunt has a long couch and witnessed that formative moment you wet yourself in a sandpit, doesn't mean you can definitely trust her advice.

Medication

We've covered many of the ways we can try to understand and manage our own mental health, but sometimes you may need some extra help. Whilst we should not jump straight to medication to 'fix' ourselves before trying to improve aspects of our lives (unless a doctor tells us otherwise), sometimes, after trying those other things, it may be something we're advised to turn to.

Our 'biochemistry' has huge ramifications on our mental health. We're all influenced by hormones, whether we're having mood swings as teenagers, or menstruating. Going through menstruation while dealing with depression or anxiety may make the hormonal effects worse, depending on the point in the cycle. And for many, the onset of the menopause brings an array of physical changes accompanied by emotional or societal connotations that can seriously affect mental health. Common chemical influences include birth control and erectile-dysfunction pills that many people take without really exploring the hormonal ramifications.

ACCESSING ASSISTANCE

The availability and accessibility of therapy, or medical assistance with mental health (and overall attitudes / openness towards it) will vary depending on where in the world you live.

If you're lucky to live somewhere with free healthcare (as we all should in this modern world of plenty), you're usually able to access these services for free – the difficult part can be availability. There can be a shortage of services in your area, or even a waiting list, which includes more waiting between any initial assessment and being seen. Be aware of this, and try to recognise when you need help and not leave it until it may be critically too late.

Private (paid for) therapy is always an option but prices can vary wildly, so it's worth doing research and looking around. Cost doesn't always reflect quality, though, and sessions will be more expensive in cases where the clinic is in a prestigious area. A £20 therapist in Edinburgh could be a million times better than a $2,000 celebrity coach in LA, so find what works for you. Sometimes costs can be subsidised, offering a discount if you're a student / unemployed / low income. Sometimes health services or governments will help shoulder some of the costs, so always investigate your options. A newer trend is for online therapy that is either just through voice, or on video, or even text. These can be cheaper and more accessible for your circumstances – just make sure you're consulting with professionals and not opinions from the eleventh page of a random forum topic. Lastly, there are many charities that offer advice, counselling and sometimes even financial support, so it's worth searching to see who can help you.

Some countries around the world still do not take mental health seriously. Either through a lack of understanding, or cultural attitudes. No matter how adverse your journey may be – if you acknowledge you need help, and try to seek it out and learn more, you are doing the right thing for your health and happiness.

If you have a deficiency in some important chemicals, medicine can assist: like serotonin deficiencies and antidepressants. Sometimes medicine is there to supplement a chemical you lack, or you may use medicine to help steady your mood, to then give you the stability to make changes elsewhere in your life to bring you back to a level where you can manage. There are also newer, more experimental drug treatments emerging – for instance some studies have shown psychedelics to be useful in cases where other treatments haven't worked. The evidence changes quickly in this area (as do medical guidelines), but it's exciting to think what we might learn and be able to treat in the future!

The most important things to mention with medication are that everyone will have different experiences depending on their biology, and that it is something to discuss with a doctor. It can be dangerous to listen to people's anecdotal experiences with different medications, so always consider things with a professional who can give you all the true pros, cons, and information you need.

There are a lot of myths around medication, mostly about side-effects and dependency. Whilst some side-effects may appear, a doctor would usually start you on a low dose and build up steadily so they can safely monitor the results – likewise, when the time comes to stop taking them, the doctor would lower the dose gradually in a responsible way, instead of going cold turkey, which can be dangerous. Don't let hearing a horror story hold you back from something you may need to help you. Hear what a doctor has to say.

I was reluctant to try antidepressants after hearing said horror stories, which told me everything from their putting people in a catatonic state, to just being a total waste of time. I went to the doctor, she talked me through the options. We discussed the plan and I felt safe and trusting of this person who is literally qualified

READ THE LABEL

Just like therapy, access to and the cost of medication will depend on where you live, both geographically and politically. Depending on the culture of your country, medicine may be expensive or hard to access, or you may be pushed to medication before trying other understood methods of managing your mental health. Across the Western world, overprescription can be an issue when medication is seen as a 'quick fix'.

Whatever you decide, you should make sure that you're checking in with your doctor regularly, so you can keep your dosage under review and consider the options for other therapies too.

It's also important to consider what other aspects of your life could be affected by taking medication. Of course your health is the priority, but things like insurance, sports and certain jobs can have strict rules on different prescribed medicines, so it is important to know and plan accordingly. As with everything, do your research and make informed decisions that are right for you.

to talk about it. At a time in my life when I was incredibly busy, overworked and not taking enough time to look after my mental health, medication helped stabilise my mood, which allowed me the time and space I needed to make my environment and lifestyle healthier. I felt less low, slightly less able to reach highs, gained a bit of weight – but by the end of the prescribed journey with my doctor I had achieved what I set out for. That was my experience, yours may be totally different. Some people use medication as a short intervention, others as a part of their daily life to deal with various physical and mental conditions. What's important is that we approach it with a reasonable mindset, not being afraid of it and ruling it out, or running towards it with too much reliance. Make sensible decisions and trust the science!

One of the biggest obstacles people can face when medication is on the table is the stigma. Through a history of humans being ignorant about mental health, combined with old science and medicinal methods, there is the stereotype of 'crazy pills'. This is completely ignorant and wrong. Antidepressants are actually incredibly common, but come with a disproportionate amount of judgement. Taking multivitamins, horrifying-aftertaste fish oil, and painkillers have no taboo – so neither should medication that helps to regulate your mood or hormones. The good news is that the world is becoming less ignorant around mental health treatments, but also more open and understanding discussing it. Someone taking steps to make themselves healthier and happier should not be judged, it should be encouraged. Don't let others' ignorance or fear stop you from getting the help you need.

Don't let a
horror story hold
you back from
something you may
need to help you.

WORKING WITH EMOTIONS

In Part 1, we covered techniques we can use to deal with overwhelming feelings that we may need to escape from in the moment, but how do we deal with feelings that persist for a while or come back regularly?

Remember that, fundamentally, emotions aren't facts telling us that bad, or dangerous, or scary things will happen to us – they are just signals that we feel something isn't right and needs our attention. They are there to make us notice a problem and push us into action. It's great when our brain fires off reassuring signals for helpful behaviours, like love, excitement or fun. Less great when we feel sad, angry or afraid. Just know that your brain is only trying to protect you – even if you are for some reason afraid of butterflies and everyone is laughing at you, your mind is making you scream in terror with the best of intentions.

A power we should all try to cultivate is the ability to sit with negative emotions. Not to run away from them, or suppress them, but to accept they are there and try to work with them, by looking for the thoughts behind the feelings. Some feelings are harder to sit with than others. Feelings like anger and shame can be particularly hard to just 'acknowledge' and 'accept' (it sounds so simple), but you can use them to see what you can change about your life to feel better.

A simple first step to getting power over your emotions is to train your ability to notice them. If you write a diary, you may have a better understanding than most people of your emotions and what affects them. It may also normalise them so it's less shocking when you feel sad, just a thing that you feel for a reason. Another great way to normalise your emotions is to channel them creatively, like a musician writing angsty lyrics or an artist painting a terrifying scream on a canvas, or me writing an inappropriate joke that I get backlash for.

I can say with confidence that as I've talked about my various emotions for people's entertainment over the years (you're welcome you vultures), I've grown more comfortable with my emotional responses and less controlled by them. By sharing the things that scare me (moths – totally legitimate, unlike butterflies), joking about what enrages me, such as the state of politics, or even just sharing a story or social incident that made me sad, I feel free and open – like a mental health trenchcoat flasher. Seeing other people relate to my tales makes me feel seen and accepted, as well as understanding myself better. My career is essentially a public diary that I feel pressured to update and where I provide salacious content for people's consumption . . . but I guess it has a good side? As well as learning not to be shocked by your feelings, understanding where they come from can help you to see what you can change in your life to manage them.

Anger

Anger comes when we feel we've been treated unfairly, disrespected, or we perceive some kind of injustice. If something clashes with your values for what is 'right', it will naturally anger you to see someone behaving 'wrong'. We base so many of our emotional responses around our 'rules' in life, and how we struggle to follow them, how adhering to them makes us feel and how well or badly things go, particularly with other people.

Anger doesn't have to be something you're scared of – sometimes it can tell us what is right and wrong and fuel us to take action. Most of the important revolutions in history came from righteous anger that sought to make the world a better, fairer place. In primal times it kept us safe as we battled for scarce resources or finally decided to fight that tiger. The problem with anger comes when we struggle to let go of it after a situation passes, or if the injustices in our life pile up so much that small situations trigger a huge angry response.

So how do you know if you're harbouring anger? Sometimes it's obvious if it bursts out, but often it might be low-level anger at everyday nuisances like road rage, or painfully slow computers. If your anger is disproportionate to the situation, and you find yourself throwing your slow computer out of the window, then that's a potential sign there's more going on – you're probably angry at something, or a lot of things bigger and perhaps more personal, and you're projecting it onto the situation in front of you. If we spy an opportunity to 'let anger out' with fewer consequences than facing whatever our biggest challenge may be, we might unintentionally release a tidal wave of rage in this

BENEATH THE BOIL

Anger is often underpinned by another emotion that may be softer, but more uncomfortable to acknowledge. Often a feeling like shame, fear or general vulnerability may be taking up a lot of emotional space, so it's easier to express or admit anger, to try to avoid a problem that's much harder to deal with. It's important to question whether there is something underlying the anger, and let yourself connect to that other feeling and work through it if you can.

inappropriate situation. If you find yourself expressing this anger towards people who may not deserve it, it's time to intervene.

If you're holding a lot of anger towards a person, or struggling to let go of it yourself, ask yourself who is helped or hurt by this anger? You'll almost always find that the person being hurt is not the other person, but just you. You lose time and make yourself feel worse while the other person goes on with their life. Learning to let go of anger when there's no way to resolve a situation can be immensely liberating. As long as you locate the root of the problem making you feel this way, you can solve it later and just try to relieve your anger physically – whatever pillow punching, casual exercising, or post-hardcore vocal recording method works for you.

The first step is usually giving yourself permission to stop being angry. It's hard to let go if we think the injustice won't go answered, or that we lose our passion or 'don't care' as much if we lose the rage. This is not the case and that's not how anger works. If you know deep down you are the one suffering by holding on to the anger, give yourself permission to let it go and you will probably be better at fixing the problem.

Just make sure that however your anger is worked out or released, you are being safe and not doing anything that will make you feel worse later. Cycling dangerously fast towards the sun probably isn't that safe, and snapping at your friends will make you feel sad.

Throughout my life, despite being notoriously non-aggressive (apparently as a child somebody challenged me to a fight and

I unironically quoted Winnie-the-Pooh and said 'sorry I'm not the fighting sort') I have felt a lot of anger. Keeping calm and cool on the surface as a survival tool through years of horrendous bullying led to pushing all the somewhat justified anger at the unfair experiences I had down, only for it to bubble under the surface. As I got older I often felt like dramatically throwing something, having a little scream, or thinking of the rudest thing to possibly say to someone. There have been times when defending myself, I've let my physical tension come out as explosively articulate verbal abuse, which even if arguably warranted in the situation, to some bigot or troll online, just made me feel like a huge ass and, ultimately, disappointed in myself. You need to let tension out in the right way and work to solve the problems beneath the boiling water. Simmer down.

Jealousy

It's understandable that we fear losing things that we love. Whether it's a person in a relationship, a promotion we're fighting for, or just a small child eating the last bit of that ice cream you've been storing in your freezer for a difficult time. That ice cream was so important and the somewhat-innocent child has definitely, totally ruined your entire day – but you can never say this. Just seethe with jealousy.

As a signal from our brains, its use is to make us aware of what we value for our survival, and to feel bad about potentially losing it, driving us into action to keep it. It can also be hugely destructive because of the behaviours it can drive us towards. If left unchecked, jealousy can make us irrational, unreasonable and controlling.

The most common scenario is the threat of another person intervening in one of your relationships. It doesn't have to be a scandalous affair, it could be a new friend joining your group, or that time you got a younger sibling and felt like you didn't matter to your family as much anymore. If that last one is you, just imagine a grumpy golden retriever that doesn't feel like the centre of attention after a baby enters the picture – you can be better than a downer dog.

The thing with jealousy is the threat doesn't have to be real. It only requires us to *imagine* the possibility in order to spiral down into a paranoid pile. When we're low in self-confidence, or under a lot of stress, we're more prone to feeling jealous as we're feeling more vulnerable.

The first step to managing the jealousy that you may feel is eating away at you, is to recognise it. We may feel embarrassed to admit what we are jealous about, but once we accept that, we can try to find what the underlying fear is. Once you know what you're really afraid of losing, you can try to reasonably consider if there's any danger. Do you need to change something to improve the situation? Or are you being paranoid, and might your actions make it worse?

It's a difficult conversation to have with yourself, but if you're honest it gives you a clearer view of the world. Our emotions often send us signals that cut through the 'truth' we like to conveniently consider – we may not want to believe we are being a bad friend, but if you start feeling jealous, then perhaps on some level you know how you could be better. It's just as hard to talk about with others, but if you discuss your feelings with the people who may be part of it, it can help if they talk you down and allay your fears. Getting these feelings out in the open (preferably in a nice conversational way – not a dramatic 'causing a scene in the bread aisle' way) can bring people closer together. It's tempting to act with anger or frenzy when opening up about jealous feelings, but if you try to catch yourself and express your feelings calmly and honestly, it will avoid making things worse, and hopefully help solve the issue you were afraid of in the first place.

It's also something you can prevent, rather than cure. It's tempting to feed jealousy by seeking out the things you're afraid of (reading messages, making underhanded comments, hoarding the ice cream tubs), but try to think beforehand about how it will make you feel. Sometimes people deserve privacy and we don't need to pry; fundamentally it won't solve the problem – so instead of just feeding the fear, try to think of a solution to it.

If you find yourself incredibly prone to jealousy, it may be that your current situations are in fact fine and the bigger issues are with your ability to trust and self-esteem. Going deeper into why you may struggle to trust, and building up your confidence and resilience, will keep you strong and able to protect yourself going forward.

Grief

This is our natural reaction to experiencing loss. It could be the death of a pet (RIP Norman the elderly betta fish) or a person we love, but also extends to other losses such as opportunities for your future, a relationship, or even just a situation you enjoyed that won't come back. It is the fear that things have changed, and cannot return to the comforting state you recognised before. Usually suddenly, we feel we have to find a way to adapt to a new life without the person or thing that we lost. It is one of the biggest shocks that can happen to our system, mentally and physically.

If you are grieving, you can feel physically exhausted and lose your ability to concentrate. It can also drain your sleep or appetite. More than the shock of learning to transition into a life without something, if it was sudden, or we are left with unanswered questions, we can find ourselves feeling stuck.

The natural human reactions to grief are different for everyone. Each person handles loss in their own way, and you should try not to compare yourself positively or negatively to someone else. Some people feel completely emotionally numb and depressed, whereas others can be totally overwhelmed by emotions – both are perfectly valid and normal responses to loss. As with other feelings, we shouldn't indulge or avoid it too much. Trying to suppress grief can quickly exhaust us, but immersing ourselves in it can take over our lives, so there is a balance to strike to begin the journey through and out of it.

For many things in life that we lose, whether it's a big personal loss or a casual everyday ending (like your favourite book reaching its last page – goodbye fictional characters that I briefly revolved my life around and considered close personal friends), we go through a process of needing to accept what we've lost. When we try to survive, usually by 'pushing through the pain', it can help us to deal with immediate difficult situations, but there will always be a reckoning. The moment of acceptance is when the emotions can burst like a dam, and it's important to have other people to see and accept how you feel. We can hold back the tears if we need to, but there is a reason crying is so hugely cathartic. Watch that movie, listen to that song. Have a good cry.

When trying to acknowledge a loss, it's important to truly see the whole picture. Try not to fixate on a single point of view, which may be a regret or a perfect version of something that doesn't reflect what you experienced in reality. It's okay to accept both the good and the bad, to remember how you truly felt and think about what your life will really be going forward. Moving on isn't forgetting or dishonouring the memory of your loss, it means you are learning to survive and it's worth thinking about how you can honour it by living a meaningful life that you can be proud of.

It's one of the times in life where you are tested hardest, and your ability to manage crises, the quality of your regular routine and environment, and your ability to cope with your emotions, will determine how well you recover. Many things can remind us of what we've lost – objects, dates in the calendar – and you can be proactive in predicting and managing your grief just like you can be with the other emotions you hopefully understand. Just remember that all feelings are temporary, and while the process may be painful, you owe it to yourself to try to go through it and make it to the other side.

Shame

Shame is possibly the most difficult feeling to bear, and can be intensely painful. Shame is more than just guilt – with guilt, we tend to judge ourselves for doing something wrong. With shame, we feel that our whole self is wrong. It's an all-encompassing sense of being flawed. Shame can make us feel unworthy and undeserving of empathy, compassion and love. Carrying it can make us very sensitive to what other people think and more likely to feel criticised or rejected.

Some of us carry shame from our childhood, if we were made to feel inadequate or inferior – or if we experience a trauma and somehow blame ourselves for what happened, even if logically we know there's nothing we could have done differently. It can also come from how we feel we fit into or are judged by society, for any aspect of our identity from race, to sexuality, or physical condition.

Growing up queer, suffering from that imposed internalised homophobia, I felt deeply shameful of who I was at almost every moment. It crushed my self-esteem and sense of worth as I felt inherently wrong – despite having not done anything myself to cause this. As a teenager, I tolerated so much exclusion and horrendous abuse, even from some people that I considered friends, because on some level I believed that I should be punished for the fact I was gay. Someone would make a casually homophobic joke in a room full of people, and instead of standing up for myself, I would hang my head in resignation. To me back then, showing an emotional reaction would have been acknowledging the uncomfortable truth I wasn't ready to process, so I just pushed it down.

We tend to keep shame a secret. This is self-destructive as shame thrives on secrecy and only gives it more power over us. It keeps us feeling under threat, and sustained for too long can develop into serious anxiety or depression as well as dangerously low self-esteem.

As with almost anything else, if you feel yourself consumed by shame for any reason, one of the most powerful interventions is to open up to a trusted person. This can immediately shed some of the shame's power. If you articulate your feelings and the experiences that underlie them, it may make you feel vulnerable – but if they empathise with you it can make you feel immediately reassured, and perhaps you can even see a point of view that makes you realise you have nothing to feel ashamed of!

It's also important to remember that even if you *have* done something to feel guilty about, that doesn't mean you are entirely

We tend to keep shame a secret. This is self-destructive as shame thrives on secrecy and only gives it more power over us.

a bad person, just as one embarrassing incident shouldn't be internalised and generalised into you being a completely defective person. Feelings are temporary and there's always something you can do to manage them, or address the situation that caused them.

Even if you logically accept that some things or events that are making you feel shameful make no sense, it can be hard to shed the feelings in a way that seems like you truly forgive yourself. This is when it can be helpful to train your ability for self-compassion.

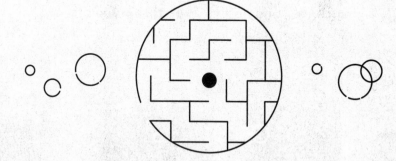

DEALING WITH SETBACKS

We all know that life can throw a curveball when we least expect it, so it's important to know how to cope with these surprises, and not let them throw you off your positive momentum.

Life is a rollercoaster, or more like the graph shape of a llama rolling down a hill and climbing up again. We can't predict the chaos. Despite our best efforts and intentions, it's normal to have ups and downs. Remember that mental health is not a straight line, we can do what we can to raise the floor level, but it will always wave with the happenings of the world.

It doesn't have to be a sudden shocking event, such as a . . . lightning strike! (sorry?) Life is naturally full of moments of change that we need to be able to handle. Breakups, moving, changing jobs – things that are very common can throw us off our track and we should all know how to keep ourselves on the rails.

Resilience

Training your resilience can help you to keep going in the face of adversity. It's more than just bouncing back, it's the act of moving forward as we grow from our experiences. Being resilient can look like:

- Viewing challenges as opportunities
- Focusing on the things you can control
- Adapting your response to challenging situations
- Maintaining a sense of purpose and drive
- Asking for support when needed

Training your resilience can help you to keep going in the face of adversity.

Resilience is about being *realistically optimistic*. It's not wishful thinking, it's just being aware of what you can actually achieve and allowing yourself to be hopeful that you will succeed. Don't be cynical about your own abilities, planting a seed of doubt that can self-sabotage. If you second guess yourself, it could be a self-fulfilling prophecy. Be realistic, but be fair to yourself and go into situations wanting to win!

It's not something that's fixed, it fluctuates through life and is something we can develop. It's partly about our mindset, but also about how we respond in the face of stressful situations. Most importantly, it's not about pushing through the pain, telling yourself you're being brave (don't hide the pain, Harold), it's about honestly accepting what you can handle and being practical. Don't overwork or exhaust yourself; it's unrealistic to expect to cope with literally everything all the time!

Think about the attitude you have when you approach situations. Let's imagine two different people being rejected after a particularly awkward first date:

- They both have similar first thoughts: 'Well that's disappointing' and 'will I ever love again?'

- But then how they make sense of that situation is different:
  - Akachi starts to accept that not everyone will love her, their date wasn't right for her anyway, and decides to take control by getting back out there and finding another fish in the sea.

– Fernando doesn't accept it, but gets stuck on the idea that they'll always be rejected, they'll never meet anyone and be lonely forever to live as a spectre haunting the local lighthouse.

• Both people are in the same situation but approach it with very different attitudes, which affects how they respond. To build up your own resilience to setbacks, it's important to understand 'adaptive coping' (see opposite).

SELF-CARE SERVICE STATION

• During stressful and challenging times, self-care is essential to maintain your overall resilience, so don't forget the basics – eating, sleep and hygiene, and staying hydrated. It may sound simple, but if you let these slip it can chip away at your hard work and your mindset.
• Try to keep your positive routine and stay on top of necessary stuff – having routine and structure gives you a strong foundation for coping.
• Take time for yourself – literally remember to breathe, be mindful if you need a moment and take time to do things you enjoy to recover.
• Protect your boundaries and don't take on more than you can handle. Don't agree to too much work, emotional responsibility, or cave in to demands you know you might not have energy for.

READING THE SIGNALS RIGHT

Psychological theory says we tend to see stressful situations in one of three broad ways: a challenge, a threat, or a loss.

1. Seeing it as a challenge → having hope, a fighting spirit and putting energy into finding a solution.

2. Seeing it as a threat → assuming the worst, feeling anxious and deflated.

3. Seeing it as a loss → acting like the damage has already been done, there's nothing you can do, and feeling helpless.

Try to look for aspects of your situation that you can see as a challenge to overcome – this will help you adopt a positive approach and channel your energy into solving the problem, known as **adaptive coping**. Of course, this might not always be possible and you can't keep fighting forever, but there will always be an opportunity for learning from the situation.

Feeling threatened is absolutely normal, but try to notice whether you're getting caught up with catastrophic thinking. Break the problem down and focus on what you can control, even if it's a small piece of the 10,000 piece 1-colour jigsaw.

If you're feeling helpless because of things you've lost, allow yourself to feel that – resilience involves connecting honestly with feelings, not shutting them off. It's a healthy part of processing what's going on for you. The key is balance.

1. Channel your energy into what you can change.

2. Evaluate any aspects bringing up anxiety.

3. Allow time to deal with your feelings.

Being flexible between these three approaches will help you deal with the fun of life's many suddenly surprising challenges.

Mindset

Mindset is everything. The mindset in which we approach challenges and life in general defines how we see things and how well we will cope. The goal is being *psychologically flexible*.

If we have a **fixed mindset**, we act as if how smart, strong or creative we are is set and not something we can affect, that our personal qualities are carved in stone from birth, and any failure is down to a lack of skill. In this mindset, seeing other people succeed can seem like a threat, our effort can seem pointless, and we're more likely to quit.

If instead we try to go through life with a **growth mindset**, we understand that our abilities can develop over time with effort, practice and support. If we see stressful situations as challenges to overcome, and failures as opportunities for growth, we will perform better. Rather than feeling threatened by others' achievements, we can look to them for learning and inspiration and see criticism as constructive.

Rather than thinking 'I can't do it' you should think 'I can't do it *yet*'. Having the right mindset sets you up for managing your own emotions better, having better relationships and performing better during any challenges in your life.

TOXIC POSITIVITY

Beware anyone who tells you all you need is a 'positive mindset' – too much positivity might be poisonous. Completely ignoring negativity in the world and avoiding difficult topics is just another form of suppression that will cause negative feelings to fester. It's one thing to treat yourself fairly and be open to growing and succeeding in the face of life's challenges, and another to just stick your head in the sand and believe all you need is crossed fingers and a wish. The balance that works is to feel comfortable acknowledging and accepting the truth of a situation, even if it's negative – having that resilient, *realistically optimistic* mindset that keeps you real, but leaves room for motivation and aspiration to get you through.

POSITIVE VIBES ONLY

This is more than just having sunny optimism in the face of an eldritch beast threatening to devour you and your continental landmass with its gargantuan unhinged jaw, there is a real evidence-backed theory of approach that comes from Positive Psychology.

Such positive language naturally scares me, but I trust science.

When it comes to setbacks in life, the way we define and interpret them will shape our response to them. So bear in mind the 3 Ps: personalisation, permanence and pervasiveness.

Personalisation – is what's happening all down to you, or *are there other factors?*
→ if you recognise what isn't your fault you can stop self-blame and criticism getting in the way.

• The hardware store I'm working for aged sixteen is closing down, is it because of that one time I accidentally pressed the panic alarm when cleaning the checkout? **No, no it isn't.**

Permanence – are you thinking that a bad situation will last forever, or can you see it as a *temporary setback?*
→ recognise things aren't permanent in order to be able to adapt and plan to tackle them in the future.

- I will never be able to act on my romantic feelings, because I am secretly a massive homo and everyone will judge me.
  Wrong – one day, I will *vigorously* act on my feelings.

Pervasiveness – does this bad situation apply across your entire life, or *just one area?*
→ think about it *specifically* to worry less, focus more and target what you want to achieve.

- I drank too much sambuca on the beach, I can never touch booze or sand again.
  Don't blame the sand, blame yourself, enjoy things in moderation and avoid anise.

Instead of seeing challenges as personal, permanent and pervasive, try to see them as impersonal, impermanent and specific. It's not a vague philosophy, but a strategy that is proven to help you maintain a realistically optimistic viewpoint and enhance your personal resilience.

Self-compassion

For the cynics like me out there, merely the phrase 'self-compassion' can make us recoil with embarrassment, but hold off – it's not being too soft or letting yourself off the hook, it's actually about being honest and treating yourself in a fair way. If you feel you carry too much shame, criticise yourself too heavily, or feel self-hatred, truly mastering self-compassion can transform how you think and feel. Even if you don't consider yourself so cynical or troubled, we can all benefit from it no matter how we feel!

Our brain's threat system, sending out all these emotions and reactions, is designed to keep us safe. However, if we spend too much time worrying, overthinking or criticising our actions, we are constantly attacking ourselves, wearing down our resilience and causing damage from the inside. Self-compassion reminds us that it's not our fault our minds do this, we are only doing the best we can with our overprotective and extremely active brains.

SIMPLE MINDED

According to the model of 'compassion focused therapy', there are three systems that affect our state of mind:

Drive – this state is what motivates us. It's all about achieving, consuming and pursuing more resources. In the past these 'resources' would be food, shelter and territory; now it is often about money, social status and a sense of achievement. Doing more and having more. When we are driven, we get a lot of our reward hormone dopamine and feel excited. This system is helpful if it's in balance with the other two, for helping us strive for our goals, but if it's extreme we can focus too much on achievement and end up stressed, burned-out and depressed. Yes, I felt very personally called out as I wrote this.

Threat – by now we hopefully understand how our minds are constantly poised and primed to look out for threats, and send us the emotional and physical reactions we need to beat them. This could be external threats like deadlines or unsafe environments, but also internal threats like being too self-critical. This is associated with stress hormones like adrenaline and cortisol. When this is in balance, we have what we need to navigate challenges in our life, but if we spend all day ruminating, this system can go into overdrive and we can overthink ourselves into oblivion.

Soothing – this system is associated with our peaceful times, when we feel safe, calm and content. When it goes into action it hits the feel-good chemicals like endorphins and oxytocin. It brings things like kindness, affection and encouragement – the things we need to feel safe. It also, importantly, softens the toxic aftermath of our drive and threat systems. This one can't really go into overdrive, unless you're so soothed you don't get anything done, and that spills over into stress? Sounds like a good problem to have.

From reading this, you may already start relating, and have an idea as to whether you tend to be slightly too driven, slightly too concerned with threats, or not good enough at soothing yourself when you need it. I've realised that I'm speeding on the Autobahn and I'm under attack. Perhaps one day when my adoloescent 'mission' is complete and I've done all the things and had all the attention and sex, I'll calm the hell down – I'm not there yet, but I like to think one day I'll just arrive. Or maybe, I just need to work on that third one.

Our life experiences tend to 'teach' us to prioritise a system if we need it – so if there was a time in our life where we dealt with a lot of threats, we may still be in that intense mode, even if we are perfectly safe now, resulting in a lot of worrying and panic. What we may need is to kick-start our soothing system. This is where self-compassion comes in.

The magic potion of self-compassion is made of three main ingredients:

1. Self-kindness – this is about being reasonable with yourself when you stumble or fail. Acknowledging your pain instead of hiding it, and being comfortable with imperfection if you know you've tried your best. Instead of judging yourself for not being resilient enough, be patient and kind. Treating yourself harshly only makes you feel and perform worse. It's not being flowery (for all you hard-asses), it's actually just being honest and fair.

2. Common humanity – as humans, we all have the same evolved brains and general experiences. We are born, we die, we struggle with the similar things and nobody is perfect all of the time, so we shouldn't expect ourselves to be. There will be ups and downs in all of our lives, so it is not something you should think you are bearing alone, and you can reach out to others for support.

3. Mindfulness – remember that you aren't your thoughts. Your thoughts are signals from your brain that are being sent for a reason. We should be able to observe our negative thoughts and feelings without giving in to and being overcome by them. Avoid suppressing them, and instead accept them and question them to find and fix the problems in our lives. If the thoughts aren't helpful, let them go.

Practice makes (comfortably) imperfect

So how do we balance these systems that drive us, and remember to practice self-compassion?

It isn't something we learn; in fact as we grow we learn naturally to be self-critical and punish ourselves for our failures. Think about how you've been treating yourself recently for anything you haven't done perfectly – are you being patient and fair? Are you being unrealistic? Are you letting yourself get carried away by bad feelings that stop you solving your problems?

We need to train to have empathy for ourselves. With painful feelings like disappointment, anger or sadness, we should step back in order to honestly consider the situation and forgive ourselves, rather than letting these feelings attack us and keep us down. Remember it's not about absolving ourselves of all sins, but just choosing not to keep indulging these feelings, even if we're trying very hard to beat ourselves up when we think we deserve it. If we hold ourselves to high standards, blame ourselves for small parts in bigger problems, or compare ourselves to others, it will be harder to develop this ability.

I was initially suspicious of self-compassion, in case (shock horror) being nice to myself would somehow rob me of my ambition. For if I am not constantly berating myself and feeling forever inadequate, where will I even find the motivation to get out of bed in the morning? This is unhelpful, and just wrong. Having self-compassion can *fuel* your ambition and make you more likely to succeed by having a better attitude with more resilience going forward. By feeling comfortable with making mistakes and learning from them, compassion can help us grow in a way that criticism can't.

SELF-COMPASSION CHEAT SHEET

- Try not to ignore or suppress your emotions.
- When talking to yourself, aim to use the same words and tone that you would with someone you care about.
- Remember we all go through the same difficulties and none of us are perfect.
- Reframe your thinking to be patient and fair to yourself, acknowledging what you've done well.
- Above all, try to accept yourself for who you are.

EXERCISE: EMPATHISING WITH YOURSELF

Good for:
- **Being fairer to yourself**
- **Fostering self-compassion**
- **Quietening self-criticism**

When you catch yourself being too self-critical, just imagine how you would talk to someone you really care about.

- What advice would you give to another person in your situation?
- What tone of voice would you speak to them with?

Then think about how you treat yourself when you're struggling:

- Would you do and say anything differently?
- And would you talk to yourself in that same tone of voice?

It's very easy to beat ourselves up and indulge in our impulse to feel bad because 'we deserve it'. The truth is that this only makes us feel and act worse! You've heard of 'treat others the way you would like to be treated':

For some of us, we need to treat ourselves the way we would treat others.

LIVING YOUR TRUTH

Looking forward, it's important for our mental health and happiness to consider what we want from life in general, and what makes us feel satisfied and ultimately happy.

Many of us ponder the great mysteries of the universe and what the meaning of it is at the end of it all – but fundamentally, we only have one life and we should try to enjoy it. Happiness is the goal.

Long-term satisfaction with life is often dependent on 'authenticity' – we need to live according to our values and accept who we are.

Values

Your values are what you find important in life, what personally gives you meaning and motivation. They are different to goals because they aren't about striving for something particular in the future, it's about how you operate and interact with the world day-to-day and how you treat and are treated by others.

If you live in line with your values, it means not just doing what you think you should do, or what others expect of you, but what you truly *want* in a way that's meaningful. It's about really knowing yourself.

Each of us has different values shaped by our culture, upbringing and experiences in the world, that define what we consider right and wrong, admirable and aspirational. These will point us forward in life as a personal compass seeking the direction we choose. These aren't the unhelpful 'rules' our minds may have, that hold us back or keep us down, they are the things that we know deep within ourselves are what we believe in and want to do.

If you aren't sure what your values are, you can ask yourself questions like:

- What do I love doing?
- What do I want to contribute to the world?
- What makes me proud?

They tend to fit into categories like:

- Family
- Career
- Community
- Health
- Spirituality

- Friendships
- Romance
- Personal growth
- Fun

Some of these will be more important to you than others. Within each of these areas, think about how you want to live your life and what stands out to you.

- With your work, do you want to be a strong leader? To contribute to your community? To be paid handsomely for your work, or to be well-liked?

- With your personal growth do you want to always seek adventure, train and test new skills or keep learning and being inspired?

- With your friends, do you want to be loyal and dependable, or fun and spontaneous?

The only correct answers are what feels right to you. It's not about being what you think society values, or what fits in with the people around you, as acting according to that would be inauthentic and ultimately make you feel unhappy. Life isn't about judging ourselves for what we value and trying to fit in, it's about learning what we truly want to do and be, and striving for it in order to feel fulfilled.

I knew when I applied to study Law at university that it wasn't what I actually wanted. It was what my family probably wanted, it's what my teachers probably wanted, and it's what I thought I ultimately wanted. I did the exams, having multiple meltdowns in the process, filed my application, and took out that big fat loan. While I was there, in my dank medieval dungeon cell with the lava lamp, I was producing some comedy on the side purely out of creative expression. I enjoyed that. I did not enjoy the intricacies of Tort in Common Law Jurisdiction, it turned out, as I was cramming that coursework to completion at 8:59 a.m. on the day it was due.

I suppose I should be thankful that, rather quickly in the grand scheme of my life (twelve months), I realised that doing this for another fifty years may not result in achieving happiness. So I dropped out, much to the transcendental horror of my family, friends, peers – and some supporters on the internet who at the very least I was counting on for reinforcement. I did it practically, by taking a year off (as I was allowed) to try to pursue something creative – and through the magical trifecta of talent, effort and luck I managed to get my foot in the door of the BBC, my videos started to gain traction, and the rest is my history. I will let you review my work and come to your own evaluation of how much talent / effort / luck featured in the balance. I consider myself reasonably lucky.

Now life isn't that simple; we can't all quit our jobs tomorrow without a plan. Reality often steps in the way of us pursuing radical authenticity, as so many things can confine us and hold us back. Cultural issues, geographic inconveniences, family obligations – in a world that requires so much of us in so many ways, sometimes we can only be as authentic as we're allowed. The current state of capitalism, as it turns out, is not conducive to good mental health. The competition, corruption and grotesque inequality inevitably leads to anxiety, stress and depression. Ask questions about the world, about your current life, and aspire to change.

If an obstacle gets in the way of you doing something you love, try to consider what is valuable to you about that thing and if you can find that value elsewhere. If you love exercise but you suffer an accident and can't anymore, consider what you liked about it. Was it the outside? Playing with friends? The rush of endorphins that I, purely based on personal experience, continue to doubt the existence of? What else could you do to bring those things into your life? You could still go outside, help your friends in other ways for camaraderie, or do other kinds of activity for the feel-good chemicals. Never assume that because one avenue closes, joy is now cut out of your life. Think about it and try to make your own path towards what makes you happy. What matters is that we recognise what our values are, strive for them as best we can, and always keep them in our minds as a guiding star.

THE STORY OF YOU

It's easy for me to have perspective on my life, as all I do is talk about myself. I actually hate it, but people won't stop enjoying it so here I am a decade later. Set me free.

Imagine someone writing the biographical story of your life – how would you want them to describe you? The way you acted? The life you lived? Your strengths and weaknesses? It can feel strange to look at yourself from the outside, but it can give you a vision of who you are right now, compared to the person you may know you want to be.

Goals

If you want to see how you can live better, following your values, you can set goals. Actionable things you can do to go in the right direction. I am loath to suddenly drop an academic acronym in the middle of your recreational reading, which I'm desperately trying to keep interesting and accessible, but in psychological circles there's a lot of talk about 'SMART' goals. When our goals are:

Specific
Measurable
Achievable
Relevant
Time-framed

… we're more likely to achieve them, and it's easier to know *when* we get there.

I can't stand acronyms, I can't stand it even more when they are good and I accept that I should remember and use them.

If you have a vague goal to 'save the whales' it might be hard to know where to begin. If you follow the 'SMART' guide you can break it down. What about getting a degree in Marine Biology? That's specific, it's measurable, it's achievable, it's relevant to whale-saving and it's time-framed which means it's tangible. Go through each part of SMART, considering if your plan is practical, makes you feel confident, and is in line with your values.

If you feel like you aren't living authentically enough according to your values, try to write down some goals, as vague as they might be, for how you'd like to live your life – then break them down to make them actionable and real.

GOAL	'SMART' GOAL
Be more sociable	Meet 3 friends for coffee this month
Help more at home	Cook for my family twice a week
Progress my career	Update my CV and send it out to at least 5 people
Take over the world	Build 17 components of my mind-controlling chip by lunch

Even if you're setting small goals day by day, if they are working towards a bigger goal and value you're aspiring to in life, it will make you happier.

Identity

For some of us, our entire identity may not be authentic. Particularly in regards to sexuality and gender identity. Continually repressing a fundamental part of who I was, out of fear and shame, kept me perpetually oppressed. If we're made to feel invalid for any part of us that we can't control, internally or externally, it creates a fundamental clash with our authenticity where we feel we aren't *allowed to exist*.

Many people try to push down these parts of themselves to avoid difficulty or danger, but as with anything else in life, avoiding authenticity will wear away at you and it won't last. For me, it was that cheeky closet, but it can be any feeling that a person is forced to betray or disagree with a fundamental part of themselves against their will. Over time we can start to believe this programming out of a desperate desire to feel accepted, but we have to push back against any brainwashing that would have us live against our values or identity.

Struggling to live truthfully in a world that discriminates against you can be a mountain standing between you and having the good mental health and happiness that you deserve. For some, it may not be safe or possible in their circumstances, so we should all be grateful for any freedoms we have and use our opportunities to create the best lives possible.

ATTITUDE OF GRATITUDE

At the end of a journey, it can be difficult,
after all the trials and tribulations, to remember
to be thankful.

Gratitude is about stepping back to look at what's around you and appreciating it, rather than striving to do or have something different. It's something that we can learn to actively practice and studies show that it has real, tangible benefits: from feeling closer to positive emotions and accessing them more easily, to physically improving our immune system, having lower blood pressure and getting more sleep. There's also the social side of sharing gratitude that makes us feel less lonely, and more compassionate towards ourselves and others.

It's more than just being thankful for the people and things we have, but making it a part of our outlook on life. If we change our perception to really see and appreciate the things we have, no matter how meagre or small, we will train our brains to notice and prioritise these positive signals. It's not emotional fluff, it's some serious science.

Many studies have shown, from MRI scans on brains, that your brain density and neural pathways can change from adopting this mindset, changing your relationship with areas like appetite, stress and sleep. These positive behaviours that your brain learns grow stronger with reinforcement as apparently 'neurons that fire together wire together' (god, nerds, I know, sorry). If we have a negative outlook on life, our brain will train that way of thinking and literally build itself to solve problems around that world view – so if by practicing gratitude we learn to look for what is going right, we actively encourage our brains to give us signals that make us feel good, and therefore make us productive and happier humans.

If we learn to feel safer and less under constant threat, our bodies are healthier. We get better at finding and producing dopamine and serotonin (the feel-good chemicals) and this creates a feedback loop of positive reinforcement that makes it even easier and more rewarding.

It's not about denying negativity or pain, or pretending 'everything is fine' when the room is on fire. It's about learning to find something, literally anything, to be grateful for even in the most dire situations. Granted, sometimes life is terrible and your circumstances do nothing to help you out – but even the act of looking for something to be grateful for can activate the regions in your brain that change your focus. That's the science, so no matter how much you want to struggle and moan and mope about the idea of looking for a rose amongst the poisonous, razor-thorned thicket that can sometimes be life, you better believe it.

When I was younger, at my lowest moment, we had a family dog. An unwanted mutt that was the byproduct of a pedigree sheep dog rogering a local collie. I loved the dog, he was an objectively terrible pet that couldn't play fetch, didn't express affection and couldn't do a single trick – but I loved him. He was useless, it was iconic. I was grateful for him. I know on some level, he kept me going.

ENJOY THE LITTLE THINGS

A basic start to practicing gratitude is to appreciate the everyday things that we take for granted, but which our life would be utterly disastrous without. The magic of plumbing giving you

Gratitude is just one more, final example of how we are in control of our mental health.

that warm shower, the hard work of two dozen bee-appendages pollinating some flowers, the reliable internet connection that powers and defines my entire existence. It's not about whispering to those flowers that you walk past – just stopping to be honest with yourself about how many comforting and contributing things are around you at any moment. Rather than comparing yourself to others or thinking about what you don't have – just taking a moment to focus on what is good and the fact it is there.

DISCOUNT YOUR BLESSINGS

Another way to train your brain into gratitude-mode is to remember a positive event in your life and think about all the things that made it possible. It's a fun one for the catastrophisers reading this, because if you imagine all the ways it might never have happened, you realise what you have. If you weren't so thirsty, you might never have bumped into the love of your life while trying to drink out of that puddle. If you didn't read that article about your dream travel destination, you would never have given yourself the papercut that resulted in you going to the hospital and being inspired to pursue your career in medicine. It might be a bit sad to imagine the hypotheticals, but remember, these things are there, you can be thankful for them, and taking the time to be grateful trains your brain to give you those feel-good signals and chemicals.

EXERCISE: BANK YOUR GRATITUDE

Good for:
- Gaining perspective on life
- Positively training your brain
- Increasing your overall wellbeing

A basic exercise to train your gratitude ability is to end the day by acknowledging a few good things you are grateful for. Review your day and deliberately focus on things that are good. It doesn't matter how mundane they may be, or how terrible the rest of the day was, if you take a moment to be grateful for something that was there then its presence in the rest of your life can be a positive reminder.

If something good happened, think about how it made you feel and *why* it happened. Think about your role in making it happen and what you can seek out to feel good again. Not only can it help assuage any anxiety creeping into your mind at night, but it trains your brain to find positives, and focus its filter on what makes you feel better so you can wake up and seize the day.

Gratitude is just one more, final example of how we are can manage our mental health. Our minds are just brains, sending signals trying to help us – but they are things we can train to help us. By breaking out of any unhelpful behaviours we've learned, and adopting a mindset that's open to growth – realistic, but deliberately looking for goodness – our minds will reward us with the energy and emotions we need to not just survive, but thrive.

Epilogue

Life is long. What this means is that whilst we shouldn't feel pressure to turn our lives around right now, we should as soon as we can because we owe it to ourselves to be happy. It's natural that on the adventure from birth to the beyond, we will experience everything we could have ever imagined, and probably a lot we didn't plan for. Just remember that your mental health will go up and down with the coming of the tides, and it is okay not to be okay.

Hopefully you feel you have an understanding of mental health, and the tools to manage it yourself, whether it's an immediate change, improving the world around you, or looking within to make a lasting impact. Just remember that there is always something you can do. With experience, you'll learn to work with your body and mind and see what techniques and principles resonate with you best. Don't wait until you're at the end of your tether to look after yourself; be aware of what you're doing and how you're feeling, and keep yourself afloat as much as you can, whenever you can.

Use the exercises in this book, think of it as your toolkit: practice your skills, and pick yourself back up if you fall. Read something, try it, put it down and pick it up to try it again when you feel ready. The point isn't that you are now forever fixed – you're learning how to get yourself back on track and what to do to keep the momentum going.

Never forget the value of support. You are not alone in this world and every one of us can reach out to someone for help when we need it. And the same applies for others: we can be that help and hope for someone else. There's no room for altruism in this mental health voyage! We gain nothing by chastising ourselves – if you do a good thing by helping someone else, let yourself feel good about it. Let's keep this ball rolling and pay it forward. Share what you've learned with the people in your life, share your story and your journey, and make them realise that all of our human experiences are (painfully) similar. You have my permission to let go of this book if you ever feel you've learned what you can and it can help someone else.

Be an ambassador for change – not like a useless politician, but someone who helps break down the stigmas around mental health by speaking up, sticking up for people, and spreading the scientific gospel that mental health needs not be mysterious – it's something any of us can understand and influence for the better. The more people who are open about how they feel, the faster we can break down the barriers, and the easier it becomes for others to open up and ask for help when they need it, instead of struggling in silence.

I've seen a lot, from confronting my mortality, to feeling I understand what it really means to be alive. There was laughter, tears, a lot of trials and even more errors – but I survived. I'm here, having learned what I can, and I hope this has helped you in the way I wish I could have been helped when I needed it.

You are never alone. You can understand what influences your mind and what you can do to make yourself feel better. If I can do it, so can you. You will get through this night.

You are never alone. You are in control of your mental health and you can make a change. No matter how dark it may get, if I can do it, so can you. You will get through this night.

Acknowledgements

Shout out to the talented and hard working team that put this thing together! Dan Kirschen, everyone at HQ and Dey Street books, eagle eyed editors Kate Fox and Rebecca Fortuin, comma-corrector-in-chief copy editor Jamie Groves, incredible and eye-inspiring graphic design from Louise Evans and Charlotte Phillips and of course Dr. Heather Bolton – whose encyclopedic knowledge and passion for improving people's mental health made this book not just scientifically-correct, but truly impactful.

Dr Heather Bolton would like to thank: Numerous brilliant friends including Jo Craig, Erin Stewart, Niamh Shanahan and Jo Barlas. My partner, Jon, for his continued love, support and encouragement. Mum, Dad and Colin, for always being there and Fiona, whose renewed commitment to investing in her own mental health makes me a proud big sister. I'm incredibly grateful to all the people who have fuelled and supported my passion for mental health so far: clinical supervisors, colleagues, teachers and mentors and, of course, the many patients who have taught me so much. Mental health is a huge topic and it's something we'll never stop learning about.